- pattern & appear true ideal.
  myself
- trust our appointme
- state problem   c
- overall empathy
- was looking food
- I noticed reliability fluctuating
- come from place of curiosity
- That's too bad.
- share our feelings
- Don't have to feel guilt when I'm sad.
- Reliability conversation.

- couples counselling.

5 love languages - Acts of service
                 - intimacy.

write a list of my needs to feel
happy in relationship:
  - free to express myself
  - Based on trust more natural & simple
  - Time together

— wants more insight & help him to help me

— This has to change, Not willing to accept this

- These are my needs. Can you do this?
- This doesn't work for me. This is what I need.

talk 2 ME²

HOW TO COMMUNICATE WITH WOMEN
TUNE-UP YOUR RELATIONSHIP
TONE DOWN THE FIGHTS
DODGE DIVORCE
AND HAVE SEX MORE THAN ONCE A YEAR

talk2ME

How to Communicate with Women

Tune-Up Your Relationship

Tone Down the Fights

Dodge Divorce

and Have Sex More than Once a Year!

by **Steven Lake**, Ph.D.

ISBN: 978-0-9879306-6-8

Softcover edition published in 2016

Cover Photo by Devin Karringten

Book Design by Jorge Phyttas-Raposo

www.**therelationshipguy**.ca

info@therelationshipguy.ca

talk 2 ME²

HOW TO COMMUNICATE WITH WOMEN
TUNE-UP YOUR RELATIONSHIP
TONE DOWN THE FIGHTS
DODGE DIVORCE
AND HAVE SEX MORE THAN ONCE A YEAR

STEVEN LAKE
PhD

WIZE
UP
PUBLISHING

Other Books from Wizeup Publishing

BY DR. STEVEN LAKE
The Sex Formula: How to Calculate Sexual Compatibility (2012)
You can order at www.amazon.com/dp/B00ATJM66S

BY KEN TANNER
*The Science of Passion, The Art of Romance: 10 Unforgettable
Scenarios to Re-Kindle Your Relationship*
www.amazon.com/Science-Passion-Art-Romance-Unforgettable-
ebook/dp/B00GGLNK04/

BY PAULETTE BIBEAU
The Bodhisattva of Attika
www.amazon.com/Bodhisattva-Attika-Paulette-Bibeau-ebook/dp/
B00ONIX9GM/

Table of Contents

Dedication

This book is dedicated to all the good guys out there who just want their partners to be happy.

Acknowledgments

First and foremost, I want to thank my life partner Paulette Bibeau who stood beside me, cajoled me, encouraged me, and kept telling me that I was a good writer in spite of how long it was taking me to complete this project. Her quiet and, when necessary, vocal support was appreciated. I don't know how or why she does it – must be love.

I would also like to thank Paulette for editing and her wonderful sister, Carol Westerhof, for copy-editing. They are two talented women with an eye and ear for how to make text more comprehensible. Thanks also to Carol Ann Fried for reading the book after publication and finding mistakes everyone else missed.

The look of this book is due to my fabulous designer and layout person – Jorge Phyttas-Raposo. Thanks to Devin Karringten, one of the youngest and hottest photographers around for the cover photo.

Finally, I would like to thank all the men I have known over the years who shared their stories with me. You inspired me to write this book. I hope it makes a difference.

Attention!!!

This book is written for men who want to improve and maintain healthy relationships with women. It is not a book on how to pick up women, there are plenty of those, but this is not one of them. This book will help keep you in a relationship so you don't have to keep trying to pick up women.

Note: *Wife, girlfriend, spouse, significant other, and partner will be used interchangeably throughout the book. Pick the word that best suits your situation.*

User's Guide

This book is like an automobile owner's manual – simple, clear and easy to use. You own this manual – you do not own your wife. If you think you own her you are in serious trouble and definitely need this book. In some parts of the world you do own your wife. You're still in trouble – at least if you want any kind of a meaningful relationship. If you want a woman who loves you and gives you succor and means it, if you want a relationship where you feel valued, appreciated and loved, and if you want a relationship where the home is a refuge and not a battlefield – then treat your lover as a person. Treat her at least as well as you treat your friends. Treat her as you would a good business partner in a successful enterprise. Because that is what a relationship is – a partnership in life. And like any good partnership, communication is a foundational skill for success.

So, how do you use this book?

1. Read it! I'm not kidding. Most men, if they read, read the paper and materials relevant to work. This book is a guide to keeping your relationship healthy through effective communication. Communication is like gas for your prized car. Without communication you aren't going anywhere. Also, in order to fix your car, set up the TiVo, or operate new software, reading the instruction manual makes a huge difference. Guys rarely read instructions. We figure we can do it on our own. Big mistake! Even if you can figure out the basics you will not get all that you can out of your relationship without knowing the finer points of operation.

Hints:
- *Use a highlighter and underline anything that is valuable*
- *Make notes right on the page, or at the end, or in a notebook*
- *Fill in the lists.*

---

2. Talk about it. Talk to your wife, your sister, your mother, and your friends. Discuss what you've read and get their opinions. Listen to what they have to say. Don't argue. Hear their side of the story. When your car sounds off you listen to the engine. You don't argue with it. The motor, if you are a good listener, will tell you what is not working. Listen carefully – your relationship depends on it.

3. Practice. Practice what you have learned. Knowing is one thing, doing is another. To get good at a new skill takes practice. To become an expert takes lots of practice. Think of Nadal, Jordon, Gretzky, or Beckham. Did you ever hear them say, "Aww, the ball/puck isn't the right size, I'm tired – can we practice later? Why is everyone out to get me?" No, not a word. They had their goals firmly in mind. So should you. Know what you want – then go for it 100%.

4. Read it again. Or at least the sections where you are having difficulty. If you used your highlighter you can re-read it quickly (another reason for that highlighter).

5. Repeat previous steps. Repeat until you are satisfied with the results. If you are not sure, ask your partner.

6. Remember this quote. When distressed about your relationship read this:

> *Love is patient, love is kind.*
> *It does not envy.*
> *Love is never boastful, nor conceited, nor rude;*
> *It is not self-seeking, nor easily angered.*
> *It keeps no record of wrongdoing.*
> *It does not delight in evil,*
> *But rejoices in the truth.*
> *It always protects, trusts, hopes, and preserves.*
> *There is nothing love cannot face;*
> *There is no limit to its faith, hope, and endurance.*
> *In a word, there are three things that last forever:*
> *Faith, hope, and love;*
> *But the greatest of them all is love.*

1 Corinthians 13:4-7

Chapter 1

WHY READ THIS BOOK?

1. You will get more sex.

You read that correctly. You will get more sex. People ask me how I can make such a claim. Easily. Have you ever seen an unhappy or angry woman want to have sex? Neither have I. What's the biggest complaint I hear in my office from women? *Men don't know how to communicate.* Therefore, if you learn to communicate, your wife or significant other will be happier and happy women want sex more than unhappy women. Ergo, you will get more sex.

Regret is a word I want you to remove from your vocabulary. Do not regret being born a man and don't make excuses for having a sex drive. The biological imperative and testosterone make you scan and assess any woman who comes into your field of vision. Admit it. Free yourself from guilty feelings that creep up on you whenever you catch yourself eyeing up a woman. Let go of those politically correct incantations that say you should grovel in shame because you lust after the opposite sex. Good for you for feeling alive. You are a healthy male. Revel in your maleness. It is your birthright. Culture, without a doubt, influences you but biology drives you.

This does not mean that you have to be inconsiderate of your wife's feelings or disrespectful of the women you are admiring (how would you like someone staring at you with spittle dripping out the side of their mouth?). You are a smart man and do not need to rile your partner or make a fool of yourself by having your chin hanging on the ground whenever a beautiful woman walks by. But, you can and will notice women. You don't, however, have to sprain your neck looking. Respect your partner and her feelings. But if she asks if you noticed, tell her the truth. Heck, she noticed! Stand in your strength while respecting your partner. Remember, your partner wants to feel like she is, in your heart, the most beautiful woman in the world, and so she should be.

And guess what? Women appreciate men who are strong and clear about who they are. My wife constantly reminds me how much this turns her on and I have heard this from other women as well. Despite all the gender rhetoric, most women still appreciate a strong man. This does not mean acting like an oversexed disrespectful arrogant ape. But as in business, strong partners are valued. And in bed this makes for much more exciting sex. That is when you can be an ape, or at least Tarzan.

2. Cheaper and less painful than a divorce.

Heartbreak, destroyed dreams, and damaged children await the families of most divorces. Don't let this happen to you. It's not worth it. Learn to communicate and save your family, your health, your sanity, and your wealth.

Buying this book will be the best investment you have ever made. A divorce is expensive, very expensive. A minimal dollar investment now could save you (depending on your net worth) a minimum of half your total assets plus court costs. And if you are wealthy – millions!

Divorces are painful. I'm sure you have heard of or seen or gone through a divorce yourself. They are typically ugly affairs where vitriol, hate and pain are the order of the day. Then there is the toll on the kids. Recent research now confirms what every parent has always known – divorce destroys a child's sense of security and trust while surfacing, often many years later, issues of abandonment. In plain English – it screws them up. If you want to increase the likelihood that your children will go through a divorce, increase their risk of doing poorly in school, and heighten the likelihood of drug usage [1] – get a divorce. On the other hand, if you want to avoid this horror story learn how to communicate with the mother of your children.

3. Stop feeling like an idiot.

When I was struggling to learn how to communicate with women I would get depressed and angry when my partner was constantly nagging at me, or calling me down, or looking at me like I was an idiot because I couldn't say what I was feeling. My negative thoughts were chewing me up. If she knew what horrific visions were travelling between the synapses of my brain she would have been truly afraid. They terrified me. It took all my energy to keep myself from acting on them when we were arguing about something important (well, it seemed important at the time). This way of being was unproductive in the extreme.

I became a "stick in the mud" unable to talk, never mind communicate. Or sometimes I'd just leave the room. Or sometimes I'd burst and start screaming at her – defending myself. All of these actions were typically met with derision, exasperation, or tears on my partner's behalf. All because I couldn't communicate what I was thinking and feeling.

When there is a lack of true communication the cost is high. Our relationships never move past these moments of unresolved conflict. You may have the willingness but not the skill to make a difference in your relationship. But what about her – I can hear you asking? What about her!??? You're the one who can't communicate. Sure, she has responsibility too. However, if you are a great communicator, which by the way means you are a good listener and *she* agrees with your self assessment, OK, then maybe she needs to learn skills as well. Since you bought this book, I will assume there are some areas in which you feel you can improve (or if she gave you the book that is a pretty strong hint there are some issues). Hey, I teach this stuff and I am constantly improving my skills. We can always learn.

4. Live longer and in better health.

Love is an enjoyable feeling. Imagine coming home after work and as you walk in the door your partner is there waiting with love in her eyes. This is every man's dream. Even if you get home first and she returns from work and as you say, "Hi darling. How are you?" She says, "Oh, it's so good to be home" and then you fall into each other's arms with a big hug and then a loving kiss feeling totally secure with one another. Would you like this? Or are you thinking, *it's been years since that has happened. I become more stressed once I cross the threshold into my home.*

Stress kills, and before it kills, you get sick. Take your pick: ulcers, bowel problems, high blood pressure, skin problems, frequent colds, depression. For most of us, having a happy home life is near the top, if not the most important part of life that we would like to have in place. Yet the divorce statistics are not encouraging. An awful lot of relationships are not happy. Look at the statistics and look at the relationships that stay together that are loveless and soulless.

I believe that unhappy relationships are a major contributing factor to men dying seven years earlier than women, having twice as many heart attacks, and committing suicide three times as often (Canadian and American Census Data). How much healthier would you be if the home were a haven rather than a battle ground all because of an inability to communicate effectively with your partner?

Life is tough. Having a loving partner to share the burden is a decided advantage. Who wouldn't want to have a partner standing beside you, shoulder to shoulder, as you face life's adversities and share the victories? Bringing up kids is a lot easier with two parents than doing it on your own.

5. Feel like a partner – not the enemy.

Connection is essential. To feel connected with your partner is a wonderful feeling. A sense of peace and rightness in the world occurs when you are connected. Two hearts beating as one. This is a wonderful goal but it's starting to sound like a romance novel. Unfortunately, for many families home is more like trench warfare with both sides dug in and very little forward movement by either side. The cost of such warfare is high. Ultimately no one wins.

As in all wars, eventually the opposing sides have to communicate in order to end the hostilities and get back to normal relations. This can be a long drawn out process or it can be quick. It all depends on your motivation level and willingness to forgive and get back in touch with what made the relationship work in the first place.

Peace in our times. Now that is a goal worthy of pursuing. So take a deep breath, screw up your courage, and be the first to go over to your partner with the olive branch and say – I want peace, would you like to work this out? Don't be surprised if there is a stunned silence from the other side. This may be so out of character that she may be in shock or disbelieving. Just repeat the question, simply and from the bottom of your heart. Because, in truth, you are tired, bloody and fed up with war in your house. So is she. So what are you waiting for? Oh right, some communication skills. That's what this book is for!

6. Improve your ability to communicate with women.

Peace in the house requires, as stated above, the willingness to communicate and work through problems by mutually acceptable means. What could be simpler? However, this simple and self-evident truth eludes even the most intelligent of us. Domestic wars often stem from communication breakdown. Or worse, from women getting fed up with the unwillingness of their partners to even attempt to listen to grievances and communicate thoughts and feelings about the situation. In other words, there has never been effective communication especially when there is conflict.

This book will give you the skills, or if you have them, help you improve implementation of these skills in your relationship. No communication skills equal an unhappy relationship. That I can guarantee. Your life will feel like hell until you learn to communicate.

In a way, if you are having difficulty in your relationship this is an opportunity. This is an opportunity to find out what is not working for you and for her. This will take a dialogue rather than a monologue which some of us are all too good at. In order to make progress in your repair attempts you will have to learn not to be defensive, to listen, to hear without rebuttal, to try and understand her point of view, and to honestly look inside and see your responsibility in the relationship.

In other words – be a man. A real man. A man who can look change in the eye and make changes because he sees the truth and values positive change. You will have to be bigger than you have ever been in your life because this is not about facing the fears of the external world, but the internal. This challenges you where your ego lives.

The upside is that if you can conquer yourself, the problems of the world will diminish before your new found flexibility and inner strength. Furthermore, you will have a new ally, your wife/girlfriend standing by your side admiring you with love in her eyes.

7. Less arguments (can you even imagine this?)

Imagine yourself in a discussion with your spouse. Yes they are discussions now, not fights. Because you have been willing to listen, to share, to face your fears and look for mutually acceptable solutions to problems, your spouse in turn does not have to make every problem a life or death issue. She has faith in you. She knows you care and will not dismiss her even if you don't understand. She trusts that you care enough about the relationship to try and figure things out as a team.

Heck, these discussions could even be stimulating. You might even enjoy yourself in the process. It's possible if you are willing to relax and have faith that you can learn these communication skill sets.

Speaking of relaxing. What would your life be like with fewer arguments? Life would be less stressful which means better health and a higher quality of life. But what would it mean for you to have fewer arguments? Write down your response somewhere because it can be used as a vision of how you want your relationship to look like. For example, *if we had fewer arguments, I would feel less uptight and angry and want to take you (your wife/girlfriend) out more often.* Do you think she might be able to support the idea of fewer arguments? You bet. Of course you can't use this while continuing your old style of communication. She will see through the ruse. She doesn't want to be arguing any more than you do. Like you, she is frustrated and doesn't know how else to deal with a situation that never seems to resolve itself. For this to work, first you share the vision and then tell her how you are going to make it a reality. Having her onboard will expedite the process. Again, she will feel included in the plan and want to support you to succeed. This has the further benefit of enhancing the feeling of partnership that we talked about in point 5.

8. Be happier with yourself.

Capable . . . what would it feel like to have a sense that you are capable in your relationship? What a wonderful position to be in where you feel capable about your thoughts, feelings, and actions regarding your partner. You would be strong within yourself and caring both for yourself and your partner. These qualities may seem in opposition when first examined but they are not mutually exclusive. The stronger you feel about yourself the more you have to give to others – including your partner.

In a sense, these inner feelings spring from the ability to communicate with your inner thoughts and feelings. The battle outside is but a reflection of inner turmoil. As the ancient Greeks said, "Know thyself." This implies the ability to commune with oneself. As you discover yourself through communication with your partner you will notice that you are better able to communicate with the world, resulting in more understanding and less conflict. This in turn will make you happier and you now present a happier self to the world which becomes a self re-enforcing cycle of good feelings and abundance.

This sounds good to me. Your partner will love it too. If you hear her say things like, "you're too serious, you're always down, put a smile on your face, you're so quiet," and the dreaded, "what are you feeling" – you need to have a talk with yourself. Once you've done that, share what you are experiencing with your partner. This will make you feel a lot better. Again your wife will feel like a partner. You will feel like you don't have to go out there and battle the monsters of life all alone. Knowing you have support will make you feel better. Learning to accept support will be good for you and the relationship. Nobody wants to hang out with a sour puss – especially if they don't tell you what's bothering them. So do yourself a favour and learn to communicate – with yourself and your partner. It'll make you happier.

9. Be happier with your partner.

Fun within a relationship is possible. Really! I know it might seem like a pipe dream from where you stand right now, but it is possible. Dream big my friend. Can you imagine what an accomplishment it would be to feel happy and satisfied with your partner? This does not mean accepting the status quo, far from it, but to get to that place where you both accept each other with all your imperfections. Now that would be a dream come true.

Of course, in order to be happier with her, you will have to become happier with yourself. There's the catch. Because in order to be happier with yourself there just may be a number of things that you need to communicate to her. Like, "I can't stand my job anymore and I need your support to see what can be done about it." Like, "making love once every two months (and it's a charity one at that) does not work for me – I feel disconnected from you and sad." Like, "I really think we should talk about our son's behavior and present a united front to help him get his life back on track."

These are conversations that require courage. It is going to take effort to change your current situation to one in which you feel good about your participation in the relationship. Out of feeling like a contributing member to the relationship you will become more connected to your partner. Out of being more connected you will understand and appreciate her more. You might even find out that you have the same concerns and are not as far apart as you thought. With these discoveries it will be easy to feel happier with her. By the way, when she sees your involvement with the relationship she will start to change as well and be more available and understanding of you. This would be nice. Yes?

10. Your home is a sanctuary – not a battleground.

Share your home with your partner. It is neither her space nor yours. It is "our" space. If you are committed to each other, the goal should be a sense that this is "our" space. This does not mean she or you will divide tasks evenly, that someone is keeping an exact count of whose money is spent on the house. What it means is that there is a felt sense of our-ness. We both feel comfortable in the space. The rest is logistics.

Unfortunately, this is not always the case. Spaces are defined as hers or mine –territoriality reigns supreme. Now if you have a woodworking shop and she has a sewing room (or vice versa) of course there will be a sense of "this is my space." I'm talking about comfortableness with being at home. That sense when you enter the house you relax and feel "at home" and not "under siege." A sense that you do not have to hide out in that one part of the house which you have staked absolute claim to – the basement, the bathroom, or the garage.

If your home is not a sanctuary, it is indicative of what is going on, or not going on, between you and your spouse/girlfriend. Tension is high. Your stomach is not happy upon entering what should be hallowed space. This is as bad as going to a job that you hate. Even more so, you have to come home every night. If this is your situation you need help and lots of it – quickly. It will either play havoc with your health or you will leave the relationship (or she will). So grab the bull by the horns, make a decision to change this sorry state of affairs and have a talk with your partner. Tell her what's up with you and that you are reading this book.

11. Learn to support your partner in a way that she appreciates.

Ask your partner what she wants. This is the only way you will find out what she needs, wants, and appreciates. Even better, ask her how she wants it. This goes from sex, to talking, to cleaning up, to dealing with the children – anything that involves her. Once again, this does not mean that you are her servant, but neither is she yours. She may want things that you are not willing to agree to. It is best if this is on the table. This is an opportunity for you to examine why you don't want to do it her way. Most relationships fail at this point. This is known in the marital field as the power struggle stage. It is a painful and noisy place to be. It could be quiet – but the tension is palpable.

When you ask her for what she wants or if you haven't and she is telling you – listen. I said LISTEN. Put away your judgments, opinions, good ideas and the remote. Listen. Really listen. Does it sound like I'm harping on this issue? Because I am. Most men are terrible listeners when women are speaking. I will talk more about this in Chapter Ten. The bottom line is to get our egos and social conditioning out of the way and learn to really "witness" what our partner is saying. To hear her in a way she has never before experienced, at least not by you.

If you can do this your life and relationship will take a dramatic turn for the better. To be really listened to is a gift for that person. Your wife will be stunned the first time you do this. The second time she will wonder what has happened to you and be concerned or suspicious. The third time tears of joy will flow down her cheeks and she will take you to bed (it may even happen after the first time but this is not why you are doing it. Right!).

When you see the results that occur when you really listen to someone, in this case your wife, you will become a believer. You will discover the joy of finding out what she wants and doing your best to give her this gift. Paradoxically, by just listening deeply, often nothing more is required. So even though you are willing to do whatever is needed, nothing more is needed. That is the power of **Deep Listening**™.

12. Greater self-understanding.

Synthesis is the bringing together or joining of divided parts and is what occurs through effective communication. Even though we know that the sum is greater than the whole we continually try to tear down our partner. She doesn't make sense, she is hysterical, and she is definitely not logical or reasonable. This is all from your point of view. What if her logic, her reasons, and her feelings had some validity? What could then be learned? If we are locked in by our negative beliefs about the opposite sex all we get to do is have our reactions. Our minds are closed to even looking at or examining a different point of view or experience. The result is that we have limited our sources of information and suffer the consequences.

Women do experience the world differently than men. If you agree with this statement then there is a whole world of experience that you know little or nothing about. Traditionally, women's experience has not been valued by men. Our worlds were separate in many ways. But that is the past. In this, the 21st century, women can and do engage in almost all areas of life that at one time were men's exclusive domain. They may even make more money than us (how does that make you feel?). Why is it that the majority of new business start-ups are by women and they are more successful than businesses started by men? They must know *something*.

This something has been identified, in part, as the ability to manage people more effectively than men. Women use their innate or learned ability to *care* to good advantage when working with employees and customers. Therefore, it behooves us men to open up our minds and at least explore the possibility that maybe our partners have something to say.

When we listen, our partners can become the greatest source of our personal growth. Believe me, this is not a fun process. I have felt like a worm on a hook more than a few times as I desperately try to avoid a truth that is being patiently explained to me even when I know that what she is saying is true. Truth does indeed hurt. But, as I learn to listen and absorb these nuggets of wisdom, or just another take on a situation, I learn. I learn in the moment about the issue at hand and most of all I learn to trust. This is a great gift I give both myself and my partner. It's a gift that keeps on giving.

13. Better understanding of women.

"Worthy goal this is" as Yoda might say. But by nature we are two different forces. The Yin and the Yang with a bit of each in the other. Unlike in Star Wars, there is no need to conquer the Dark side except within ourselves. Both men and women are designed to come together (no pun intended but how could I not notice. I'm a man), to join in a union that is greater than the individual. Out of this joining we learn about ourselves and set the stage for procreation. A miracle.

But to really understand women, that would be another miracle that

I'm not sure I can deliver. It is like trying for perfection, a good idea that keeps us going in the right direction. Just don't get hooked on it or it will be your demise. We are human after all and perfection is an unattainable illusion.

Learning to communicate with women will, however, give you way more understanding of their wants, desires, needs, and world view. This will make you the envy of most men because they will see women talking to you and cooing about how thoughtful, intelligent, and caring you are (all because you know how to listen – if nothing else). They will envy your relationship with your partner because she talks to women and men about how wonderful you are. They will notice the loving smiles you exchange at parties from across the room and how you go home arm-in-arm with smiles on your faces. Yes, you will be grudgingly admired by your male friends and hailed as a unique specimen by your female friends.

You will learn a lot about women, not everything, because we can't know what it is like to have a period or to give birth or to know that a man could force himself on you and to have to be vigilant when most men wouldn't even think about personal safety. Most of us will never know what it is like to walk in high heels (though we could find out) or be constantly appraised and judged on our looks. No, we will never fully understand their moods or mysteries. And that is part of the attraction. For if women were like us, then they would be men, and I would rather they be women.

14. Learn successful behavioral patterns.

Death is constant, life is change. So why are we all so busy trying to protect the status quo? It's a losing battle. I love this quote by Bettin Arndt, "*Women marry men hoping they will change. They don't. Men marry women hoping they won't change. They do.*" Arndt has pretty much summed up how many relationships are played out. We all know some woman who is convinced her man could be amazing if he just listened to her. And we all know (you may be one) some guy who is shaking his head in disbelief ten years after the marriage wondering what happened to that sweet innocent girl he walked up the aisle with on his wedding day.

Flexibility is the name of the game. In my practice I see many men who are unwilling to change. They don't want to make the effort. Typically, they feel *she* should change. They ignore their alcoholism, their depression, and their verbal abuse. It's her problem. And at one level they are right. She is sticking around. Why? Because she loves him and is hoping against hope that he will come to his senses and make some changes – and occasionally it does happen. Usually, it is too little too late and many couples coming to marriage counseling are actually seeking divorce counseling.

Recently, a client of mine "got it." His wife was going to leave if he did not learn to communicate and have a meaningful relationship with her and the kids. He realized what was at stake, woke up, and applied his considerable talent and concentration on learning a new way of being. It was stunning to watch how quickly he shifted. First, he made some mental re-adjustments, and then he changed his behavior. He made mistakes, but now he knew when he made them, and if he didn't, his wife would point them out. He listened even when he was raging inside. His courage to learn and change was inspiring. This story always gives me hope and reminds me that change is possible.

Communicating his experience to his wife was the key to success. The skills in this book are what I taught him and many others. If after seventeen years of feeling separated and resentful of his wife he could learn to change, forgive, and accept her reality (she gave no guarantees of staying) you too can learn and receive the rewards that await men who can communicate with women.

15. Find hope.

Communication comes first. It may be having a serious talk with yourself, your friends, your therapist, and ultimately with your partner. But talk you must if there is to be hope. The most frustrating and difficult problem I have when working with men is that they don't want to talk honestly about the issues. It's kind of hard to figure out what's bothering them if they won't communicate. Likewise, you too must screw up your courage and take the plunge. This book will give you some guidelines, tips, skills, and encouragement; but ultimately it is up to you. You must open your mouth and say your truth no matter how awkward or painful it is. Remember the old saying, "The truth shall set you free."

If you are new to relationship and are reading this book to get a head start and not take twenty years of painful learning, good for you. However, you still have to practice. Reading is only the first step. You don't even have to be in a relationship at the moment. You can practice with your sister, a female friend, your mother. Ask questions, then listen and learn. Take note of reactions. Watch your interviewing technique. Do you interrupt? When do you interrupt? When does the conversation seem to get boring? When is it easy to participate and when is it difficult? When are you comfortable and when are you uncomfortable? What beliefs do you have about women and how do they affect your relationships?

Also, observe people in relationship. What works and what doesn't? Ask your male friends, if they haven't already told you, ask where their relationship works and where it doesn't. They may look at you in a funny way at first but persist with sincerity. Say that you want to do it right, you want to learn how to have a successful relationship. They will give you one side of the story. Make sure you talk to the other side. It may not be appropriate to talk to your friends' girlfriends or wives in this manner – it could cause problems and strained relationships, but do talk to women about what they want in a relationship. It will be an eye opener I can assure you.

When you are in a relationship, remember, it is only through action that anything gets done or changes. So, take action today, now, this moment and commit to changing your relationship for the better. Learn to COMMUNICATE!

Summary:
The reasons to read this book are:

- You will get more sex
- You will learn how to be effective in a relationship
- Way cheaper and less painful than a divorce
- You will stop feeling like an idiot in the relationship
- A happy marriage will increase your longevity and make you healthier ?
- Being able to communicate with your spouse will significantly reduce the stress in your life
- You will feel like you have a partner, not an enemy
- You will learn specific communications skills
- You will have fewer arguments
- You will be happier with yourself
- You will be happier with your partner
- Your home becomes a sanctuary and not a battleground

- You will learn how to support your partner in ways that work for her
- You will learn more about yourself as you engage your wife in open and honest communication. You will learn what your buttons are, how to overcome them and how to give and receive love. Being in a relationship allows you the opportunity to explore yourself in a way that is not possible on your own
- By learning to communicate with women you are learning new and successful patterns of behavior
- By learning to communicate you are bringing hope back into the relationship. A relationship without hope is a sad thing. By communicating you are demonstrating a willingness to go beyond despair and take action for a better tomorrow.

Now that you know the reasons to read this book, lets explore the differences between men and women.

Chapter 2

DIFFERENCES BETWEEN MEN AND WOMEN

No one will ever win the battle of the sexes;
there's too much fraternizing with the enemy.

Henry A. Kissinger

The obvious differences – physical

I love talking about the differences between men and women. It seems so clear. Just look at us. It's obvious that we are different. She has breasts. Well, OK, so do you and I but they look very different (unless you are taking progesterone). You've got testicles and a penis – she doesn't. And our body is a different shape. Men are broad shouldered, women have a narrow waist. On average, women are smaller than men in height and weight with corresponding differences in strength – men are stronger than women on average.

These obvious visual and physical differences have been made out to seem as if we are talking about two different species. On the genetic level, nothing could be further from the truth. Chimpanzees and humans share 95-98.7% of the same genes according to Barry Starr, a geneticist out of Harvard. These figures keep changing as new studies are completed with a downward trend in the similarity between chimp and human. Likewise, recent research from Britain's Sanger Institute in Cambridge demonstrated a 1% difference between individuals of the same genetic material. Men and women share about the same (98.7%) depending on how you count (genes or base pairs). So if you want to say that you have more in common with a chimp than with a woman, somehow I don't think women will argue with you. In geneticist terms, it is quality not quantity that determines differences and similarities and in these terms we are indeed closer to our sisters than to the apes. Genetically we are almost the same. Out of 20-25,000 genes for a human being there are 78 genes that are different between men and women. So how come women seem so different from men?

Well, biology accounts for some of these differences. Having a menstrual cycle and all those hormones coursing through her body has an influence. This is an obvious one that we are familiar with. The biological differences start earlier than adulthood. Girls seem to mature (physically and some would argue emotionally) earlier than boys. Girls scoot ahead height wise until boys are in their mid-teens when they catch up and then exceed their female peers on height and weight. There is evidence that girls have brain differences as well [3]. This is evident in their ability to learn language skills earlier than boys. This may be due to the way girls interact with each other which places a heavier emphasis on language skills.

Emotional

Babies are great especially when it comes to emotion and emotional expression. When they are sad or hurt they cry. When they are happy they smile and laugh. When they are angry or frustrated they pout or scream. Their feelings can change in an instant. They don't hold onto a feeling for long. They have one emotion and then they have the next one. An infant rarely says, "Gee, I was angry at Mom for cleaning my face so I'm not going to feel joy now that she is kissing and tickling me. No siree, I'm going to sit here and get depressed about her controlling behavior." Infants don't think this way. Teen-agers do, but that's another story.

Men have feelings. This may surprise some of the female readers but we do. We may not show them easily, but we most definitely have them. *It is in the showing of feeling that men and women are radically different.* How is this so given that we were very similar when babies? You guessed it. We have been conditioned differently.

What was the first thing you remember as a young boy about emotions? This is universal in North America and many other cultures – "Big boys don't cry." Think about it. There you are, 3 years old, you've tripped over a toy, scraped your knee and Daddy says (it's almost always the father), "Hey you're a big boy now, and big boys don't cry." And you look up to your Dad who you want very much to be like, and even though crying seemed to be alright for the first three years of your life – not anymore. So, you gulp back and swallow your cry, wipe the tears from your eyes even though your knee hurts like hell, you say, "OK." Dad then says, "While you're at it, wipe the snot from your nose." Just the way he says it makes crying not only childish, but humiliating as well.

Granted, not all dads may have been this harsh and yet some were harsher. "You want to cry, here, let me give you something to cry about," and then you get a whack upside the head with his hand. Ultimately the message was the same – don't show your emotions. *Crying says that you are weak and vulnerable.* And we learned to squelch other emotions as well. Sometimes we were ridiculed for laughing too much or too hard. At other times it was for smiling in a certain way. "Wipe that smirk off your face or I'll wipe it off for you." And for heaven's sake don't act silly or your age. "Grow up," must be a universal phrase taught at Parenting School.

But it was not always the verbal assaults that had the most effect. It could be the disapproving look by either parent or the snickering of older boys because you wanted to play a game that was now deemed too young. I learned to hide complex emotions like disappointment, sadness, enthusiasm. Overt enthusiasm was seen almost as a sin. Such uncontrollable natural expression of energy seems to threaten the very existence of many fathers.

What emotions were washed out, dampened or disapproved when you were growing up? Please, take the time to make some entries in this list. It is the first step in practicing communication.

Unacceptable Emotions When Growing Up

1) _____

2) _____

3) _____

4) _____

5) _____

On the flip side of this issue are the emotions that we are allowed to express. Typically, men are free to express anger whereas women are free to express sadness (crying). This is a broad generalization and each family and the culture at large teaches us what is acceptable. Have you ever been around construction gangs (I worked in construction for years)? You hear lots of anger. Everyone seems angry and there is a constant barrage of swearing and insults. I've never heard anyone say "You're hurting my feelings," or "Let's change the atmosphere around here and make it more supportive and positive." No. Anger was the norm.

In professional or office situations who gets angry and lets off steam? It's the boss, the lawyer, and the doctor; most of whom are in positions of power and typically male. If it is a woman getting angry she risks being labeled a bitch, controlling, and over-compensating. Not that co-workers don't have harsh words for an aggressive and abusive male boss – they do. They are just more willing to put up with it when it comes from a man.

In some environments the expression of emotion is highly controlled. Even crying by women is unacceptable. There is a hospital story that demonstrates the male/female divide and the hierarchal setup in medicine. A patient had died and the female nurse who had been caring for the patient was charged by the male doctor to inform the relatives of the death. She did so and was crying with the grieving family. The doctor happened to see this and was outraged telling her that she was being unprofessional and must control her emotions.

In this example we see the need of the man to control a natural expression of sadness after a death. If we can't express emotion at such a time when can we? It seems that some men are extremely threatened by the expression of emotion. In the corporate culture it is seen as taking away rather than adding to the work experience.

The historical explanation for this is simple. The world of business was created by men for men. The rules of emotional expression were understood. Strong emotions that motivated others (anger/threat) were acceptable and weak emotion (sadness/crying) that portrayed weakness and presented oneself as vulnerable (like women) were to be avoided. This worked fine until women joined the workforce in large numbers and became problematic as they entered management.

Men are supposed to present themselves as controlled. Even though anger is allowable it is not as highly regarded as the controlled man with his emotions in check. Nothing gets under his skin. Drives women crazy! They know you are feeling something and they want to see it. So what do they do? Start pressing every button you have trying to provoke a response. What do you do? Try to stay in control even more as you are getting more and more pissed off. We've all been there. Either the man walks out or he loses it and explodes, ending with a, "Are you happy now?"

She is not happy that the issue is not resolved but she is happy to see that you have some feelings and that you are indeed human and not a robot.

Spiritual

The most obvious spiritual difference that jumps out when I think about this question is that men tend to run most of the religions that I know about. They seem to have a lock on Christianity, Islam, Hinduism, and Judaism and a host of other religions. The Catholic Church will not allow women to be priests, rabbis are men except in some of the more liberal branches and mullahs are men. Some of the Eastern religions like Buddhism, Hinduism and Taoism accept, in theory, women into the priesthood, but in practice this is rare.

Patriarchy, or men in power, is the norm in today's world. This was not always so and at one time the priestess was a powerful spiritual presence in the community. Things have changed in North America, and to a lesser extent in Europe, with the dynamics between men and women radically changing over the last 30 years. In North America, women today comprise almost half the workforce [4]. As women come into their power through gaining control of their finances and procreativity they are examining their relationship to male dominated hierarchies.

More Research on the Differences between Men and Women

Before listing all the differences between men and women that are supported by academic research I have a few words of caution. Researchers are human beings with all the same foibles that you and I have. They are affected by fads, by money (i.e., research grants) and by what publishers want (getting published is very important to a researcher). They have reputations to build and to protect. They also have political agendas though few if any would admit to this. The most egregious example of this is the debacle with global warming data originating from England. Every few years in any branch of science or humanities someone is caught fudging the data to advance a personal belief.

Academics can indeed be lost in the proverbial ivory tower and have realities that are different from the common man. Twenty five years ago it was believed (in academia) that divorce had no ill effects on children. Every parent knew that this was absurd. Unfortunately, academia conveniently ignored the parents' reality and political agendas were part of the reason family researchers ignored the obvious. The academics did not want the harm done to children in a divorce to be used as a reason for women not to get a divorce and stay in an unhealthy marriage.

Today, those same researchers, to their credit, have reversed their stance on this issue and have the research to prove their new point of view which just happens to be what everyone knew twenty five years ago. The upshot of this is: trust your ability to weigh and include in your calculations data that has, as we say in science – *face validity*. The data must make sense on the surface or we have to seriously re-consider its relevancy. That being said, enjoy these research findings. And remember – things change.

The brain

At one time, the fact that male brains were bigger on average than female brains was used as evidence that men were superior. Then someone asked the question, "but are not men bigger than women (on average) and could this difference account for brain size?" And sure enough, when we match for weight, the data changes. Except for newborns, 3-12 year olds, and people over 86 years old, females have bigger brains [5].

Here are some more differences, and as usual in research, some of these findings have been questioned:

- The inferior-parietal lobule is significantly larger in men than in women. This difference may account for men being better able to manipulate 3-D objects [6].
- Two areas of the brain that are involved in language processing, Broca and Werniche's, are larger in women than in men which could explain superior language abilities in women [7]. This is another chicken and egg issue. Are these areas bigger at birth or do they develop through usage? There is also an interesting cultural difference. In cultures that use non-pictographic alphabets (e.g., Western), men have a left brain bias and women use both hemispheres more equally when processing language. In cultures that use pictographs (i.e., Eastern) both men and women use the two hemispheres equally.
- Men have more neurons in the cerebral cortex while women have a more developed neuropil; this is the space between cells thus allowing more synapses, dendrites and axons. And what does that mean? Better, faster and more efficient communication between neurons is what it means. However, on the up side

for men, having more neurons allows us to be less obviously, or more slowly, affected by dementia as we have a functional reserve compared to women [8].

Research on boys and girls

There are lots of interesting findings about differences between the sexes and these differences start early. For example [9]:

- Even at day one in infancy there are differences. Girls look longer at faces and boys look longer at suspended mobiles.
- By 12 months baby girls respond more empathetically to the distress of others.
- By the age of seven, girls are more able to judge a potentially hurtful statement (or maybe boys have learned to ignore potentially hurtful statements or at least not respond to them).

Dominating behavior and establishing hierarchies vs. co-operation and caring for the relationship are the main findings from research [10] that examines play styles of boys and girls. The games that boys use when playing together are qualitatively different than that of girls playing together.

Boys tend to play in larger groups and the point of their games is to determine hierarchy. Who is the strongest, fastest, and most courageous? Girls on the other hand tend to play in smaller groups, two or three at a time, talk, and take pains to down-play differences in ability, making sure that the relationships are not disturbed by any uncomfortable feelings brought up by differing skill levels. Boys, on the other hand, will point out their superior skills, brag about it, and be admired by others for their abilities. When playing, boys will actively challenge others, constantly seeking to move up the hierarchal ladder.

Note: *When girls become teen-agers they exhibit more competitive behavior.*

Communication

These different play styles also affect how boys and girls communicate. Boys use language to communicate status through bragging and displays of knowledge. Boys are learning to use talk to emphasize status while girls use talk to emphasize connection [11]. These styles affect us as adults. Women tend to downplay their expertise [12] and male experts talk more than female experts. In fact, when a female expert was paired with a male non-expert the men, on average, attempted to dominate the conversation and challenge the other for control and status. As in the child studies, women tended to downplay their expertise and not use it as a source of power as the men did.

Other differences in communication styles [13]:

- Men use "I" when women use "we".
- Men toot their own horn more than women and women believe that if they do they will be disliked.
- Men minimize their doubts and women downplay their certainty.
- Men see asking questions as being in a "one down" position and thus lose face. Men may also form negative opinions of those who ask questions in situations where they would not.
- Men avoid apologies as it puts the speaker in the "one down" position. Women say "I'm sorry" more than men. No kidding.

It drives us crazy. The interesting thing about why they do is that women don't see it as taking responsibility for the event but as a way of showing empathy by saying they are sorry that it happened. Their intent is creating support and connection whereas when we hear it, we take it literally and think they are apologizing and we are confused or irritated because we know they are not responsible for the event – so why are they apologizing?

- When receiving feedback it is more effective for men to be given one message. The process favoured by women, of softening the blow by first telling the recipient what they do well, then telling them the areas to change or improve is lost on men. Men will focus on the first half of the message and downplay the second half. They will leave the conversation thinking that there is no problem.

- Through competitive games and teasing while growing up, men have learned to battle hard for a point while arguing but not take it personally. Women experience this verbal assault as reflective of the relationship and take it personally.

- Men talk to create status, women talk to create connection.

- Men are better at negotiating pay raises [14].

- Men make more statements and women ask more questions [15].

- Men use minimal encouragers at the end of statements to indicate agreement; women use them throughout to indicate they are following the speaker [16].

- In male/female dialogues men interrupt women more often and change the topic more frequently [17].

The results of a poll conducted on a marriage advice website [18] debunks the notion that sex, money and who helps out most around the house are the biggest marriage problems couples face. Of the 207 women participating in the poll, more than 40 % said the single biggest frustration of their married lives was that their husbands "didn't communicate enough." This survey confirms what I have heard in my office over the past twenty years.

Health

Hey guys, I have some positive information for a change (well, sort of). This information is from the Institute of Medicine of the National Academies [19]:

- Less men than women die of heart disease every year but we start having heart attacks 10 years earlier than women.
- Men are from a third to a half as likely to get depression as women (that may be because we don't go to see therapists as readily as women so this may be under-reported).
- Men comprise only 20% of those suffering from Osteoporosis.
- Men are more successful at quitting smoking, have less severe withdrawal symptoms, and suffer less cardiovascular problems from smoking than women.
- Men are half as likely to contract STDs as are women.
- Men make up only 25% of autoimmune disease sufferers.

Like I said, it's a mixed bag. And now for some more uplifting news . . .

Longevity

In the developed countries of the world men live four to seven years less than women. For a long time this was attributed to genetics. We just lived less long. More recently, the idea of men living more stressful and dangerous lives has surfaced, putting into question the idea that we are inferior (regarding longevity). Men have way more accidents, engage in dangerous sports, commit suicide more frequently and succumb to violence in greater numbers than women which lowers our longevity.

When you add into the mix having to support a family (though nowadays it is so expensive to live both the man and the woman have to work), the demand to have a "communicative relationship" with the kids and spouse, having to appear successful to the world, and coping with the stress of work – it is a killer and carves years off our lives.

Just how bad is it? Up to age 60, risk-taking behavior claims more lives than circulatory disease for men [20].

Education

There has been a lot of controversy over the years on how boys and girls learn, are treated in schools, and biases in teaching favouring one gender over the other. At first boys were being favoured (remember, throughout most of history girls did not attend school) and so an effort was made to be more aware of this bias and support girls in academia. Now it is girls who are being favoured and our boys are falling behind. Both sides, and there are sides in this debate, have advocated for the separation of boys and girls in education. We've been down this road before and people who can afford it often make this choice. The oft cited reason for separation is that both sexes can concentrate better as they are not trying to impress each other. Also, girls don't have to play dumb in class as appearing smart can lead to rejection by the boys. This last tactic is not limited to girls. One of my nephews deliberately suppressed his marks on exams so that he would not be seen as an academic nerd to his friends.

Here are some research examples around learning and education [21]:

- When it comes to processing speed as determined by timed tests, boys and girls were the same in kindergarten and pre-school but then girls leapt ahead in elementary school and maintained their advantage throughout middle and high school.
- Males have higher drop-out rates in school.
- But then there is an interesting finding that shows boys being better at completing verbal analogies and knowing antonyms and synonyms.
- And even though there are these differences, the intelligence of boys and girls is the same.

Nurture vs. Nature

When it comes to the old nurture/nature debate, I believe we need to start out with an elemental fact – men have a Y chromosome and women don't. As much as we share genetic similarities we also have this glaring difference that cannot be ignored. How far reaching these 80 or so unique genes make us different from women is the focus of much research and speculation. Some of these differences are obvious to the eye (literally) and some are much more subtle; like the different ways drugs interact with men and women and how symptoms and diseases are expressed.

Another difference resulting from the Y chromosome is the chemical soup that we produce in our bodies. We have much more testosterone and this hormone makes us different; stronger in some ways and weaker in others. It makes us more prone to violence, Autism and Asperger's disease, and risk-taking (not always a bad thing).

I have discussed some of the early childhood research demonstrating differences from birth (what attracts baby boys' attention) and differences in the brain. However, the brain differences cannot categorically be assigned to nature as the brain is plastic and these differences may be the result of or be influenced by nurture. There is a lot of argument in this field of research.

Research on identical twins has shown that genes can be turned on by the environment. This is the conclusion reached when, for example, one twin develops Schizophrenia and the other doesn't [22].

No doubt nurture affects personality development and yet, as any parent will attest, those kids come out the chute with a well-defined personality. Maybe well-defined is not the best phrase but a strong personality that gets refined over time as the child interacts with the environment.

The point of all this is that there is a great deal of variation within Homo sapiens and between men and women. This variety should be celebrated rather than made the focus of dissention and separation between the sexes. Yes we are different and yes we share similarities and yes we can change, learn, and grow throughout a lifetime. All that is needed is the desire. Your biology will not hold you back. However, your personality will if you are not willing to change.

Summary:

Our five senses tell us that men and women are different. These are the obvious differences that stand out and can be easily agreed upon. Many of the arguments that occur over the differences between men and women revolve around whether certain differences are genetic (nature) or the result of the environment (nurture). These differences of opinion tend to occur on subjects like intelligence, abilities, and drives or how we act in the world. Genetically we are almost identical. However, that tiny difference looms large in the real world.

I believe that men and women are similar when it comes to emotions. We both have them but men have been trained in radically different ways in how and what we express. Essentially, boys have been taught to repress certain feelings especially those that are seen as feminine.

Spiritually, men are in the dominant position as we control the religious aspects of life through patriarchy. There are some changes occurring due to the women's movement, education, and the ability of women to control whether or not they get pregnant. This is mirrored somewhat as women move into more visible roles within their religions.

We need to be careful when examining the data as researchers are people with their own biases and prejudices. Researchers tend to find what they are looking for and academic journals overwhelmingly publish positive results so disconfirming results are often not submitted which skews the perceived reality.

An example of this is research on the size difference of male and female brains. Bigger was seen as better. Recent research demonstrates that there are differences with males being superior in some ways and females in other ways, but on overall intelligence, there is no difference.

The research on boys and girls shows that some differences occur even on the first day of life, with girls more attentive to faces and boys more interested in mobiles. As boys age they become less empathetic, more physically aggressive and establish hierarchies based on dominance.

As boys engage in group activities they learn specific communication styles which enhance status. They toot their own horn, minimize doubts, appear knowledgeable, avoid asking questions and appearing in a one down position.

Health-wise, there are some advantages to being a man and some serious disadvantages. Bottom-line, we die earlier than women. We have more accidents, engage in dangerous sports, commit suicide, and die by violent means more frequently than women. These are some of the contributing factors to our lower longevity.

Differences in our abilities, as determined by research on the brain, are reflected in education and learning. Typically, girls are better in verbal processing and timed-tests and boys have the advantage on three-dimensional-rotation of objects in space. There is however, no difference on overall intelligence between boys and girls.

Even though there is much argument in the academic community about whether certain differences between men and women are due to nature or nurture there is one undisputable fact – men have a Y chromosome and women don't. This little guy (58 million base pairs compared to the X chromosome with 155 million base pairs) creates some major differences in how the male diverges from the female of the species.

Now that we have identified some of the differences between men and women let's examine *how* we became the way we are.

Chapter 3

HOW DID WE BECOME THE WAY WE ARE?

You have to evolve to stay involved.

Steven Lake

Evolutionary psychology – it's in the genes! (If silence is golden then why does it irritate my wife?)

Justification of presently unacceptable behavior seems to be the raison d'être for evolutionary psychologists. Some of their writing makes them sound like apologists for traditional patriarchal ideals, couched in scientific jargon, and hiding behind the parapets of academia. If you examine who is involved in this research area you will find few if any women. This should be a hint that something is amiss. It is a male dominated branch of theoretical belief trying to explain the behavior of Homo sapiens based on the principles of evolution. These writings sometimes come across as an attempt to excuse gender inequity.

Now that I got that out of my system, let's examine some beliefs held by evolutionary psychologists. The one I find most amusing is their take on how men became less competent in the verbal arena. The story goes like this. In the old days, before the dawn of civilization, men were hunters. As they went out to catch their prey it was quickly discovered that silence was important. Being talkative could result in scaring off the prey or being eaten by predators. Men that were chatty got eaten and over the years, through natural selection, talkative men were removed from the gene pool.

Meanwhile, back at base camp, women were looking after the children and co-operating with other women in activities where communication was important. This led to enhanced communication skills, development of empathy and nurturing activities.

At one level this sounds reasonable. Except, we all know plenty of men who talk too much. We wish they had been eliminated from the gene pool. And women complain vociferously about how men do nothing but talk and don't know how to listen. The evidence of everyday life goes counter to the theory.

Evolutionary psychologists seem to be regurgitating the dualistic issues of the old nature/nurture debate. The majority of opinion in behavioral science is that behavior is a complex interaction between nature and nurture. Nature gives us some qualities that are set and some that are only predispositions. Nurture gives us channels or paths in which natural predispositions can be expressed or even sublimated.

A powerful example of this is a tribe in Indonesia where the women dominate and the men act in a feminine way – they cook, care for the children, and gossip – while the women work, deal with finances and control the direction of the future. What we consider typical male patterns of behavior are *not* expressed universally and the evidence shows it can be substantially modified. According to Bailey and Peoples, across cultures there are no biological differences to explain the division of labour [23]. Furthermore, Ryan (of *Sex at Dawn* fame) writing in Psychology Today stated that:

While EP (Evolutionary Psychology) offers a valuable way of thinking about psychological development and life in the prehistoric environments, many of the most prominent voices in the field are less scientists than political philosophers. They choose some aspect of modern life and construct elaborate justifications located in an inaccessible ancient environment. Often, the fact that their story seems to make sense is the only evidence they offer. [24]

That being said, if you believe in evolution, it does make sense to me that the demands of being human and our relationships with women are influenced, to some degree, by our biology and our evolutionary process. Men and women have different physical, chemical/hormonal and genetic attributes that affect how we interact.

History: A man's job description throughout the ages

History has a way of being told by the victors and to their advantage. The current history of the male/female war has depicted men as the winners. Feminists and history tell us that men have been the privileged ones and it's hard to argue given that women, until recently, were considered property – men's property. Yet, in the end, class may be more reflective of power than is gender. Men, like women, feel helpless, powerless and frustrated by circumstances. Men (and women in some countries) are the ones who go to strange lands and die for the ruling elites. Are we in the same position as women? No. Does being a woman add another burden on surviving? Yes, I believe it does.

But I am jumping ahead of myself. Let's look at our traditional roles as men. Provider, protector and law-giver come to mind. In the beginning, we provided by gathering and hunting (women also contributed especially in the gathering of food). At some point it seems men left behind the gathering and focused on hunting. This changed again when planting of crops occurred in climates favourable to agriculture. Yet, there seems to be a mythology where man-as-hunter is seen as the ideal. Much more exciting images come to mind such as the thrill of the hunt, the kill, the dangers surmounted and the victorious welcome when we return home. Farming is nice – just not exciting. Even today we describe the work place as a jungle with all it entails.

How did man get the label of provider? Women provided as well, they collected food and certainly today bring in the bacon like men. The inherent biology of women as the bearers and nurturers of life has led to the label of caregiver. In traditional cultures, being a caregiver did not mean you did not provide as well. Even today, many African women are both the major source of the household income as well as the chief care-givers [25]. Somehow western civilization and our attendant mythologies have separated these two functions completely – provider for men and caregiver for women.

Armies are not a natural outcome of organized groups. However, the early Egyptians (about 5,000 years ago) are a good example of the militarization of a culture. They were one of the first societies to use conscription [26]. Males were seen as fodder for the war machine and women as factories that produced the fodder. At that time, major changes in society were established by decree that separated men and women's experience of the world into distinctly opposite realities – creators and destroyers – where previously they had shared in the joint venture of survival and procreation. In a sense, our biology was professionalized or mechanized. Maybe this was the beginning of, at least for men, an alienation from the forces of creation and from ourselves. For women, this became disempowerment through loss of control over their bodies – it now served the state. Both sexes however, were victims of powerful ruling elites. This is the model that ran the world, and still does for the most part. With the advent of the pill and women regaining control of their reproductive capability, the world changed.

Women today make up 49.6 % of the workforce in the United States [27] which means that both sexes are providers. What about protectors? How much physical protection does a woman need in the industrialized world? Not as much as in the old days, yet the powerful male is still idealized in advertising and in the gym where males still develop powerful bodies to impress women. Arnold Schwarzenegger lives. Fortunately, for older or less strong males, we have a highly controlled society with protection by the police and power emanating from factors other than brute strength. The formula of success in high school no longer rules. Information, intelligence and money are the steroids of modern man.

What is defined as strength may have shifted yet we (men) still protect through our power. We protect those who are seen as weaker – women and children. We still default to seeing women as physically weaker (which on average they are) and many women tell me they want to feel protected and encourage, whether consciously or not, the desire in men to protect. This puts men in a bind. There are a lot of mixed messages out there. How to negotiate your desire to protect with respect for the equality of women and their messages that support traditional behavior is tricky and requires an assessment of each woman you are interacting with. What's worse is that most women are probably unconscious of the mixed signals they are sending. It's enough to make you pull your hair out.

The element of law-giving shows up in the home for the average man. This is a reflection of how, until recently, all law-givers were men. Even today the formulators of law are dominated by men. In the home men are called upon to "lay down the law," make judgments between fighting children, and mete out punishment.

Stress of life (Why does stress kill men before women?)

Violence, or the potential for violence, is a part of every man's experience from childhood onwards. We have all heard stories of men being violent in bars (and anywhere alcohol is available), baseball parks and rugby fields. When in a potentially dangerous situation, say walking your partner home late at night after a national holiday, there is always the threat of violence. You are on guard and most men, whatever their age, are prepared to fight if necessary. This is a reality we live with. It is not about ego, it is about survival and protecting our loved ones.

Life is full of stress for men and women alike. According to Canadian and American Census Data, men:

- Have 1.5x as many cancers as women
- Have 2x as many heart attacks as women
- Have 2x as many ulcers as women
- Commit suicide 3x more often than women
- Get murdered 4x more often than women
- Have 6x more on the job accidents as women
- Get arrested for drunkenness 13x more frequently than women
- Die 4-5 years earlier than women.

This sucks. Society talks up a good game about the advantages of being a man but when you look at the above list, there is a high price to pay for these so-called advantages. How did this happen? In the science of differences between men and women there are theories about how women have superior physiologies. They are hardier, withstand pain better and have better endurance. But maybe there is something else at play. Maybe the life men lead is simply more dangerous to our health.

We know unequivocally that stress reduces the immune response, over-stimulates acid secretion with attendant stomach and bowel problems, raises blood pressure, disturbs sleep patterns, and puts pressure on us psychologically. Do we have more stress than women? This is a difficult question to answer as it is subjective. I think we can say the modern world is more complex than earlier times and possibly more stressful (though living in the Middle Ages and dealing with the Bubonic plague might have been a tad stressful). The destructive forces of our war machines are immense and pervasive. Life is more complex and gender relations have gone from a time when there were strict and clear rules of engagement between men and women to now, where what is appropriate seems to change every five years. Today there are vast differences in the composition of the workforce and integration of women into jobs that were exclusively male is well under way. There has been some migration of men into traditionally women's jobs, like nursing and elementary school teaching, but this is still the exception rather than the rule.

Men are expected, still, to be the major bread-winner. Women who make a lot of money tend to go out with men who make more. There is an unwritten rule, or understanding, that when a woman gets pregnant she can choose to take time off and be supported while bringing up their child, whether it is for a month, a year or until the child enters school. Many men prefer this arrangement seeing it as in the best interest of the child. Not all women take this route. Some go back to work as soon as possible. Generally speaking, however, most men find it stressful having an extra financial burden.

Men work harder when there are children in the family and might take on another job or push for a raise. This leads to less time with the spouse and children, which usually leads to the wife expressing her concerns and dissatisfaction with her husband thereby creating more stress for the man. This process can go on for 20 years or more. In my practice, I see men who are baffled when their wives suddenly announce they are leaving the relationships saying they don't know their husbands anymore. He has been too busy with work. Hearing this he becomes confused. He thought he was doing what a man is supposed to do – working hard for his partner and children. This is stressful. Very stressful!

What about at work? We have seen that men do work differently than women. Men are brought up to compete and women to co-operate. Which do you think is more stressful? Always being battle ready, in a heightened state which engages the fight or flight syndrome eventually burns us out. The body is not made to sustain this chemical and hormonal priming without the physical release that is not possible in modern work settings.

If men had, like women, social networks in which to share concerns and stresses, maybe there would be better outcomes for men. We don't. The average guy may have a couple of good friends, a larger group of sport or drinking buddies, but they rarely talk about their problems. It goes back to showing weakness or vulnerability. Want to get a guy squeamish, ask him to be vulnerable and share feelings. He'll either laugh at you or puke. This gives you some idea of where we are coming from. So, we keep it in and pay the price.

Demands of being a man (the 3Cs)

Confidence, competence, and control are the masks men show to the world. These masks serve only to perpetuate a mythology of the strong individual who can battle seen and unseen foes on his own. Again, the cost is high as these qualities are masks only and are not internalized. Sometimes the illusion is so complete men forget they are wearing a mask until a crisis hits. That's when we fall apart. That is when we start drinking, or becoming abusive, or falling into depression and refuse to get help.

What is it about control that is so alluring? This control is in reference to the external world, which, if we examine it with any clarity, we see as inherently uncontrollable. But we do our best to control it anyway. This is natural to some extent as we're talking about survival here. Yet, the control we can most easily apply is over ourselves. I can study hard so that I pass my exams with good grades and can then apply to college with the expectation of being accepted. Makes sense to me.

And yet, people get all twisted and bent out of shape when they can't control the behavior of *other* people. My wife, my children, my parents, my employees never seem to do what I want. This is endlessly stressful. In order to cope I put on the mask that I am in control of my world. I hide my inner experience. We become, in psychological terms, *incongruent.* This split between our inner and outer selves is the stuff of great stories like *Dr. Jekyll and Mr. Hyde, Star Wars,* and our endless fascination with spies. Spies present one face and have a whole different world existing beneath the surface appearance. What is the cost? Can we be honest with anyone if we cannot be honest with ourselves? Does the habit of wearing the mask become so habitual that we forget we are wearing it?

Control and the need for control are easily shattered. Your child dies, an earthquake destroys your home, or you are hit by a car while riding your bicycle; these events shake you to the very core. The illusion of control dissolves and an existential angst slips in upsetting your concept of what the world is and should be. This can be devastating. And it needn't be a life and death event – lose your job after 24 years one year shy of retirement and it becomes blatantly obvious that control is an illusion.

Along with control, men must appear confident. Give me a break. We are all just boys in adult bodies. Now I have to appear confident as well as in control. Sure, sometimes I feel confident – it's a great feeling but it only lasts a short time. The main purpose of confidence is to show the world I am on top – not one down. People will feel secure in my presence and want to associate with me. Most importantly, they will not try to take advantage of me because if someone has confidence they have power backing them – or so we think. And people respect power and are more likely to fawn over you than attack. Confidence feels as great as it looks.

Control and confidence are creations of the mind with no substance beyond their projection or experience as a feeling. Competence, on the other hand, is measurable and real. You either have a certain skill or you don't. If you don't have competence, this can be dangerous as you will then have to fake it. You truly do not have the expertise you should and you know it. This would be a cause of stress. Being promoted to your level of incompetence is truly cruel and unusual punishment. It's also bad for business.

Advantages of being a man

Respect is a wonderful feeling. I expect to be respected by those around me whether I'm at work, the supermarket, or at home. As a man people acknowledge my presence. This is not always so with women. Women have told me how they can be ignored in conversations that include men and it is not always obvious. It can be a gradual and subtle shift of focus to the men in the group and the women being excluded or seen as minor players.

Other advantages include:

- There are more men in the boardroom than women
- Shorter line-ups at public washrooms
- Don't have to worry about looks and hygiene to the same degree (though that has changed for the younger generation)
- Less worry about walking alone late at night
- No fear about being physically beaten up by your spouse (though this does happen, and not because men are weaker, but because they are afraid of hurting their spouse, these men are taught never to hit a woman, or are afraid of being assumed guilty by the police if they are called to intervene)
- Not automatically seen first by your gender and then by whom you are
- Grey hair adds status
- Not dependent on your partner to open up jars or do tasks that require more strength than the average woman has
- Your last name stays the same (unless it gets hyphenated)
- Getting ready in the morning or going out for the evening takes less time
- Sexually experienced men don't worry about "their reputation"
- Haircuts and many other services and products are cheaper
- You can take your shirt off on a hot day
- People don't glance at your chest when you talk to them.

And if you want to have a good, though politically incorrect, laugh, go online and check out "advantages of being a man." The above list is by no means extensive; being a man has its rewards and will as long as we live in a patriarchal world.

In God's image (Why do men have a sense of rightness and superiority over women?)

Belief that we are doing the right thing gives us energy. It feels good to feel certain. When I don't question myself I am clear, focused and nothing can distract me from my goals. I have this unquestioning faith when I believe I am right about something, when I am backed up by the beliefs of others, when I am backed up by established systems, governments, academia, law or religious texts. Knowledge from on high is a powerful aphrodisiac.

The bible, and many other religious texts, state that we men are made in the image of God. Women, on the other hand, were made from one of our ribs. They came into being through us by God's hand – whose image we are made in. And, since the advent of patriarchy, women have indeed been second to man. But it gets worse; she is to blame for our downfall, our alienation from God (the apple story) and should be subject to our scorn for her inability to resist temptation.

Here is the part that really gets me; she is then blamed for successfully tempting us and yet there is no mention of our inability to resist her temptation. It is as if we are helpless before her – go figure. If your wife cozied up to you, batted her eyelashes, and told you to buy that million dollar house would you? OK, OK, maybe you would.

My God this is sad. We can't even accept responsibility for our actions. We see ourselves as fallen from grace almost like our greatest foe, the fallen angel himself. What other mischief can women get up to? We have to be on guard all the time lest they lead us into temptation. No wonder we have trouble talking to them as we are suspicious of women from the get go. They are different and untrustworthy. Needless to say, this doesn't predispose us to effective communication with women.

This may account for some of the pithy utterances you hear from women, like: "Who do you think you are . . . God?" or "What gives you the right to order me around?" or "Hey buddy, don't tell me what to do," or "Who do you think you are, God's gift to women?" If any of these sound familiar you may want to do a reality check and examine your beliefs about women. Do you believe that you, as a man, are inherently superior? Do you believe women should do your bidding? Do you believe you are smarter – just by being a man? Any of these beliefs will get in the way of effective communication. How did we get this way?

What we learned at home.

Open your mind to this statement. *Very few of your beliefs are yours.* That's right! They were given to you by your primary caregivers, usually your mother and father. When you were a baby, that innocent and empty mind was a sponge soaking up everything they said and believed. You just wanted to be like them and, not having the maturity to examine their beliefs, swallowed them whole. Maybe, when you were a teen-ager, you started to question their beliefs – maybe not. And even if you did, what do you believe today? Do you treat your girlfriend or wife like your father treated your mother? Who did the dishes, the laundry, swept the floor? Are you replicating your family values without awareness or are you conscious of what you believe? And more importantly, are these beliefs nourishing the relationship or harming it? If you are not sure ask your partner.

Examine your beliefs and test them against your behaviors. You may believe in equality but if all your key workers (whom you hired) are men that might be indicative of underlying belief systems. It is important to open up and dissect our beliefs to see what we like, what we prefer and what irritates us and why. This examination can lead to deeper understanding of the choices we make in life as well as understanding why we react to certain things women say. What happens when a woman challenges you, insults you – what do you take as an insult? How do you respond? Is it with violence, withdrawal or a reasonable dialogue?

Here is a list of people and systems that drive values and beliefs deep into our minds.

- Mother and father
- Brothers and sisters
- Extended family members
- Teachers
- Friends
- Media
- Religious leaders
- Political leaders
- The prevailing cultural beliefs which are usually transmitted by the above list.

Let's make a list or chart of your beliefs regarding women. Then examine when you started the belief and who gave it to you. Lastly, ask yourself if the belief is one you want and if it is conducive to effective communication with women.

My Beliefs About Women

Belief	Since when?	Who gave it to you?	Do you want it?	Is it effective for communication?
Example: You should never hit a girl/woman	5 years old	Dad	Yes	Yes
1)				
2)				
3)				

Doing vs. Being

Action is what makes most men tick. We live for action – action movies, action videos, sports, and sex. Action can be experienced directly or vicariously. Either way we love action. We are sensual animals. Movement is intrinsic to Homo sapiens. The thinking man is designed to move as well as think. To move his hands, his arms, and his legs. To throw, grab, squeeze, pull, push, and hammer. If we do not move our bodies we are not happy. Sit at a computer all day, and even if you enjoyed the work, your body feels like crap.

Men in society get their value by what they create, or more specifically, what they produce and get paid for. This has its advantages and disadvantages. We end up creating a lot of stuff. Our society is a wonder of mechanical and technical inventions and innovations most of which were created by men. We can send a man to the moon and back again and we have eradicated numerous diseases that caused untold suffering throughout history. These are a few of the miracles we have wrought. The downside is that these creations take a lot of time and energy. This work,

71

this doing, becomes a mistress that takes us away from family and friends if we are not careful.

Yet, even knowing this, the pull to do is so strong that few can resist. You feel the accolades and approval from your parents when you get a good job. Our partners are happy we can contribute to the larder in bountiful ways. Indeed, the survival instinct has to be honored and doing a job appeases this drive. But what happens to the need for a happy intimate relationship, the need to bring up our children, the need to contribute to our tribe or society, and the need to look after our body which is so easily ignored?

It is as if we only have one need – to produce money by doing. As you can see, if we are so focused on doing when do we get time for being? By being, I mean existing in a state where we are connecting to ourselves and others and not doing activities that separate us from ourselves and others. We are being with our wives, talking and listening, sharing our hopes and dreams, telling funny stories and making love. We are teaching our children about life through stories about Granddad and Grandma. We are walking with them in the park or forest, pointing out the wonders all around. We are being in touch with our spiritual nature. All of these activities help develop our character and enhance our personality. We become richer in spirit. Ultimately, by developing our inner world we develop the ability to communicate with self, our spouse and God (however you conceive him/her to be). Otherwise, you're just a boring paycheck.

Habit and change

Habit is what keeps us from making change. Habits are strong behavioral patterns ingrained at a neurological level. Changing these patterns requires repetition – burning in new neural pathways. What habits am

I talking about? All the ways of thinking and being that do not support effective communication with women. Men have been in a privileged position in many ways and this privilege has handicapped us in our relationships. It will take effort to change.

That's the bad news. The good news is that the brain is fairly plastic and can indeed learn new behaviors [28]. We will have to avoid short term gain to avoid long term pain. This is tricky. We see the chocolate cake and want it . . . now. We see the football game on TV and want to lie on the sofa . . . now. Stopping and thinking if these actions are moving us towards long-term goals is not natural. We move on our impulses. Our passion or feelings make our choices and then we justify our choices with logic and reason.

You are up against all the years of your life that you have lived to this moment in time as you read these words. As mentioned earlier, first we must identify our beliefs. What works and what doesn't. In Chapter 12, I go into greater detail on how to uncover self-defeating behaviors in our communication styles. We cannot always see our behavior and this is where another pair of eyes comes in handy.

You may be battling what your peers believe, what your religion says, and what the culture at large dictates. **Deciding to communicate with women as equals is a radical act.** You will be applauded by some and derided by others. But in the end, when you have learned how, you will have the last laugh or should I say smile, because you will be happier, your heart will be full of love, and you will be getting way more mutually enjoyable sex than your ignorant friends. Here's to change!

The Women's Movement – get over it already!

Threatened by the Women's movement? Give me a break. Are you so insecure you fear some change? Are you a wuss or a man? Life is change. Adapt or die, that is the law of nature. If you are too lazy to listen to the complaints from your partner and take the time to honestly see if there is any merit to what she says, and at the very least acknowledge her feeling – she should throw you out. She is your partner not your serf.

At the beginning of the book I said that you should treat your wife at least as well as you would treat a business partner. And you would listen to your business partner if he or she had a major issue. You certainly would do whatever it takes to correct the situation because you don't take your business partner for granted. You know it will make working together untenable if the issue is not addressed. It is the same with your intimate relationship. If the issue is not addressed the house will burn. Maybe not today, but eventually – guaranteed. If it doesn't burn down you will be made to suffer so much you will wish it had.

Here's a tip to throw any Feminist off guard. *Listen*! When she, or on rare occasions he, starts off on a rant about something – don't argue. No matter how outrageous you think their statement. Simply *listen* then ask questions in a non-mocking and non-derisive tone. And then *listen*. Repeat until the conversation is exhausted and then thank them for their point of view.

This technique serves two purposes. One, you will determine if the person has a reasonable position or is a fanatic, and two, you might learn something. Yes, you may even change your mind about some previously held belief. This is perfectly acceptable. You are not losing or being put in a one down position (because you have only asked questions they will not know you have changed your belief about a certain point). You can't lose. If they happen to ask about your beliefs you can share them or gracefully say that the speaker's discourse will take some extended thought and time to digest and you have no reply at the moment. Then, thank them again. For your personal enjoyment, take note of their response. They will probably be speechless.

Life experience – does what you know make a difference? (Why do men have a tendency to deny or ignore the state of their intimate relationships?)

How old are you – twenty, thirty, forty, fifty, or more? Are your beliefs about women the same as they were when you were younger or have they changed over time and because of your experiences?

I idealized women and put them on a pedestal. I had a close relationship with my mother and learned to talk to women through engaging with her on a regular basis. My mother did the cooking in the house and hated it. But she did it. Interestingly, all my past girlfriends cooked for me – and loved cooking. Even my wife cooks for me. I am a lucky guy. Did I plan it this way? No – at least not consciously.

The real problems with women came when I expected them to be like – you guessed it – my mother. I expected them to be energized, intelligent, interesting, physically warm, a good conversationalist, and concerned about my well-being. As I write this I realize a) what an incredible woman my mother was and b) how difficult it was for my partners to live up to this hidden agenda I had for them (unbeknownst even to me).

Because I was sick for much of my childhood, I got a lot of attention from my mother. I like being the centre of attention even to this day. My wife on the other hand hates the way I complain about all my aches and pains and does not reward this behavior with attention.

I try to please women waaaaay too much. I had trouble breaking up lousy relationships. I think this was because I believed they were above me (on the pedestal) and I must try to please them lest they leave. I wrongly believed, until my mid-thirties, that I had to take care of a woman's feelings even at my own expense. I was also gutless. I was not able to be truthful and stand the pain of leaving.

In those days I would rather endure torture, until it became so painfully obvious to both of us that it was over – either she would leave or it was a mutual decision. I rarely left first. This character flaw lasted until my mid-thirties at which time I finally matured enough to realize I did not need to allow myself to be abused and would survive just fine after losing someone I loved.

And that is how experience has affected my relationships and beliefs about myself and women. I am stronger, wiser, and have more courage to say and do what is needed. I am certainly able to express my anger at women (something I had real trouble with). Now I can communicate all my thoughts and feelings in an assertive manner and support my partner to do the same.

I still think women are incredible. I love them. I love making love to them. I love hanging out with them. I also like hanging out with the guys and there are some things I talk about with the guys that I don't discuss with women. Yes, I get to hang out with women. Not all guys have this opportunity. Fortunately, my wife isn't jealous very often, and when she is I quickly reassure her.

TIP: *Do not argue with your wife if she is jealous. Listen to her, reassure her, and examine your behavior to see if you are a) flirting in front of her, b) snapping your head when a woman walks past, c) giving way too much attention to another woman, d) gazing into another woman's eyes or touching her, or e) ignoring your wife when in the presence of another woman. If you do any* *of these activities – STOP. If you don't do any of the above activities and your wife is insanely jealous – get help fast.*

Family (Why men need to walk the talk around family – we say it's important but focus on work to the detriment of the family.)

Family values are hard to keep if we are at work all day and into the evening. Or if we work all day, come home to eat then disappear into the computer for three hours. If you want a family you have to *participate*. You have to participate with your wife, children, friends and relatives. Family is composed of a constellation of relationships and relationships take time and effort. Typically, men have not been shown how to communicate effectively and there is no manual to follow (up till now) so we make a lot of painful mistakes as we try to learn about women and ourselves.

I never felt like killing someone I loved until I was in an intimate relationship. This is serious stuff. How could I, in that moment, come within a hair's width of taking an axe to my then girlfriend as she came down the stairs screaming at me? The only thought that prevented me from grabbing the axe and striking her – and feeling good about it – was that I wasn't going to go to jail for that bitch (sorry if the language offends anyone but that was my thought at the time). It scares me to know what I am capable of. And it gives me great peace of mind to know I can control a killing rage and make a choice that ultimately took care of me and my girlfriend.

Fatigue, stress and a lack of support make being an effective partner difficult in the extreme. In order to battle the realities of everyday living we must become conscious and see that the current social order is stacked against us, not only for effective communication, but also for effective relationships. You have to be the originator of change. You have to take the great leap forward and say, *this has to stop, I am not willing to do what my father did, or be like my buddies, or do what my culture expects, or blame the past for what I did not learn.* No! You have to make a statement to the world – *I change now.*

Then, as Tony Robbins says, you must take "massive action" to create what you want. You will also need massive awareness of your thinking and habitual patterns of behavior. Finally, practice on a daily basis is what leads to massive new behaviors.

The Influence of Culture

We are molded by the culture in which we grow up. As I have mentioned earlier, there is the family culture, but that is embedded in the larger culture – the culture of the region and the culture of the nation. The prevailing beliefs of the time influence your beliefs whether they are transmitted by radio, TV, or the internet. Often these messages were in direct opposition to what your parents were trying to teach you. My early years were a time when many teenagers actively questioned their parents, moral teachings, and belief systems.

The average person is bombarded with hundreds of advertisements each and every day [29-32]. Your beliefs about what is attractive in the opposite sex may well be influenced by this. Did you read Playboy or Penthouse or view porno on the web? Do you watch TV and see the portrayal of beauty in all its mesmerizing allure? Beautiful women are used to sell countless products and from this ingestion of multi-data streams we unconsciously compare the women in our daily lives to these airbrushed mannequins. And we wonder why women get angry when we compare them (not slim enough, not sexy enough, not as put together enough, etc.) to these art director creations. We even have TV shows that take your ordinary female and do a makeover and turn her into the woman of our dreams. Like all of consumer society, the goal of the producer is to make us feel inadequate in some way so that we will buy their products and feel better. Unfortunately, this is only a temporary fix and we have to buy, buy, and buy in a never ending search for beauty, strength, status, well-being and happiness.

Now that I have hit you over the head with my rant about the consumer society let's examine how culture has affected your beliefs. Do you date women of other races? If not, why not? Do you date women of other religious beliefs? Do you date strong women or subservient women – why and why not? Do you date women who make more money than you? Again, why or why not?

Peers (Why do men find it difficult to get support from peers?)

Is there a male friend or a group of male friends that you can talk with about the issues you have in life? If so – great! But if you are like the average guy, you probably don't have the same sort of intimate relationships with your peers that women do.

I remember my father. He was the lone wolf. He didn't even have any deep relationships outside my mother. He had friends who were usually male co-workers but I never saw him even going out with the guys. If you do go out with the guys, whether for bowling or playing baseball, what is the quality and depth of conversation you have?

When talking about difficult subjects (e.g., sex, death, relationships, and kids) most men, in my experience, use humour and jokes to manage these issues. Nothing ever gets too serious. Heck, that would be boring. And please, don't get emotional unless you are crying into your beer. Then we say, "Yeah, Steve was crying last night but he was drunk – must have had one too many." And if you do this regularly, "Steve has a problem.

Thank God it's only when he drinks."

I believe the reason men in North America find it difficult to have a serious conversation about our difficulties when talking with other men is that we do not want to appear weak. It puts us in a one down position and goes against our competitive nature and our culture of self-reliance. Also, we have not been trained to share feelings with anyone and certainly not with other men. Being intimate with other men can bring up homophobic issues as well. Watch how men are with each other physically when the conversation steers toward emotionally laden topics. They will again use humour or get physical. A rough hug, a punch on the shoulder or a slap on the back – anything to bring the other guy out of his feelings – is how we deal with emotions. Encouraging further discussion by asking probing questions or giving solace by touching is avoided. Have you ever seen a man take another's hand and say, "I know how you feel. Tell me more."? I am laughing out loud as I write this because it seems so not the way it works. With a woman yes, a man – no.

The world has changed in the last twenty years. Men were watching Oprah (31% according to Quantcast on Sept. 28, 2010) and are aware of the cultural shifts that have occurred and are still occurring between men and women. More men than ever are taking advantage of their Employee Assistance Program (EAP) and Employee and Family Assistance Program (EFAP) programs to take counseling when having difficulties either at work or at home.

When I first started counseling twenty years ago very few men were my clients. This has changed and there appears to be fewer stigmas for men to go to counseling. I say this with great caution as this trend is more reflective of urban populations over rural – where there may not even be access to counseling – and with men with advanced education, and less so with immigrants who still carry old-world-beliefs that are similar to those of my father's day. The idea of using a counselor or psychologist is foreign in many countries except for the most severe mental disturbances. And maybe that is still the thinking for many men, as women still access mental health care more frequently than men [33].

Brothers and Sisters

There is a lot of debate about the influence of birth order on personality. But I think it is reasonable to say that having, or not having, siblings affects our personality development. How could it not? If you have siblings you either learn to share or fight for what you want. If you are an only child, not only are you the centre of attention but you don't have to think of others or share anything. Also, the eldest child is often given responsibilities like looking after the younger siblings, whereas the youngest may become used to being looked after and always told what to do. Being younger means being less physically and mentally developed and more at risk of being bullied by older siblings. Whether you are the eldest or the youngest child, the relationships you have with your sibling will affect your view of the world.

I have a friend who had five sisters and he was the youngest in a family of eight. Did the five sisters and being the baby affect him? Darn right. He is very comfortable with women and knows how to get babied by them without breaking a sweat.

Then imagine growing up as a single child. You never have to share anything. Hopefully you are getting your parents' undivided attention. Of course, that can be a problem as well. You may become the centre of their universe and end up with a God complex or believing that everything should revolve around your needs. If your Mom or Dad was a single

81

child there are no cousins, aunts or uncles. If you and your wife are from one-child families your children will not have aunts or uncles – so much for an extended family.

Much is learned from our siblings both good and bad. A study by Laura Argys [34] found that younger siblings between 12 and 17 were more likely to smoke cigarettes, drink, and use pot. Younger siblings between 14 and 17 were more likely to be more sexually active than their older siblings. After controlling for race, ethnicity, socioeconomics, and family size, she stated that younger siblings are prone to risky and delinquent behaviors and this is attributable to birth order. Argys believes this is due to initiation of age inappropriate behaviors by their older siblings and by worn-out parents who are not as vigilant in their parenting as they were with the first child.

If you are interested in birth order I recommend the works of the famous psychologist Alfred Adler, a contemporary of Freud, who was the first psychologist to spread the concept and importance of birth order. More recently, Frank Sulloway writes about the effects of birth order in *Born to Rebel* [35].

Summary:

Genetically and culturally we are the sum total of all those who have preceded us. How you interact with the opposite sex is both genetically encoded and taught. Evolutionary psychologists attempt to understand and explain current behavior by examining the evolutionary functionality of behavior stemming from pre-historic adaptation processes.

One change that has occurred recently is how we define ourselves – what it means to be a man. Not so very long ago men were the providers, protectors and law-givers. What it means to be a man is evolving (at least from a cultural perspective) as women gain access to previously restricted areas of society (work and education), acquire financial independence, and control of their reproductive capacities.

It is obvious that men and women are different in many ways. Is it nurture or nature? There are the obvious physical differences (nature) and then there are the differences that are learned (nurture).

Unfortunately, men die younger; having more cancers, heart attacks, and ulcers than women. We commit suicide more often, get murdered more often and have more accidents on the job. Is this due to nature or a reflection of the different demands placed on men (nurture)? Or is it an interaction effect between nature and the environment?

Many cultures demand that a successful man display confidence, competence, and control. This expectation also creates stress that is often managed with drugs or alcohol which leads to all sorts of social problems and depression in men. Despite all these challenges, being a man has plenty of advantages. Many of our advantages have been handed down through time. Our laws and religions reflect the fact that we live in a patriarchy. We get instant respect and are usually listened to when we talk.

Your life experiences affect how you think about and deal with women. Each relationship you had made an impression on you, and either confirmed or challenged previously held beliefs. As you enter into a relationship with a woman and live with her, this is either the greatest opportunity for personal growth or a glimpse into what hell is like. It's up to you.

In order to become aware of how you operate, understanding that men's tendency is *to do* rather than *to be* is critical. And when you take time *to be*, your relationships are enriched and so are you.

There are many factors influencing how we think, what we believe and how we act. Some of what we learned growing up has value and some of it doesn't. Once we are aware of these influences we then have the option to examine them, and if we choose, to change our attitudes and beliefs. What was taught can be untaught. What is habit can be broken, and new habits instilled into our thinking and behavior.

Chapter 4

THE CHANGE PROCESS

The need for change bulldozed a road down the center of my mind.

Maya Angelou

If changing your behaviors were so easy, you would not need this book. Change is difficult. We are chained to our habitual patterns for good and bad. It is as if, once set, there is reluctance in our psyches to get behind change even if it is good for us and we desperately want to change. Old habits do die hard it seems. In this chapter I examine the change process and what you can do to effect change. Let's start with a visual representation of the change process known as the "Pyramid of Change."

PYRAMID of CHANGE

Change is the end result of a process. The process involves:

1) Problem recognition
2) Motivation to change
3) Examining Values and Beliefs
4) Skill acquisition
5) Life practice

Let's examine each of these in turn.

Problem Recognition

Problem Recognition is the first step. If you don't see or admit to having a problem, why would you fix it? This seems obvious on the face of it but it is surprising how people will avoid facing their problems. It is as if you can make it go away or wait it out if you don't confront it. This tactic is often used by those who don't like conflict, feel they are too busy, or believe it is her problem, not mine. On this last issue let's be clear. *If she has a problem – you have a problem.* Remember, you are partners. Her experience affects you and the relationship. If she is unhappy, believe me, eventually you will become unhappy.

Motivation to Change

Motivation to change comes next. You would think that if a problem is identified the motivation would follow. Not necessarily. You might think it is not such a big problem. Or, you might think it will go away on its own. Or, you might not know how to deal with it. Or, you feel you don't have the energy. Or, _____, fill in the blank. Essentially these are just excuses to avoid stepping up to the plate and dealing with the problem. Even if you don't believe there is any hope of fixing it, better to work on this now than later – it only gets worse the longer you delay.

We tend to be motivated if we are excited or in great pain. These two extremes run our lives. We move towards pleasure and away from pain. In relationships, however, we often have to move first towards more pain to get more pleasure. Confronting an issue is painful yet it is the only way to get to the pleasure. Keep your focus on the end goal, pleasure, and that will help you engage and cope with the pain.

Another way of looking at it is to focus on the negative end result. If you don't engage the problem, all hell will break loose and it will cost you big time. You can avoid this problem by engaging and communicating with your partner. You are avoiding the bigger pain by engaging in the smaller pain.

Examining Values and Beliefs

Let's assume you have recognized there is a problem and are motivated to change. Seeing as you bought this book, or someone bought it for you, you might as well examine your values and beliefs. Examining values and beliefs are vitally important because every thought you think and every word you utter is influenced by your values and beliefs. If you believe it is OK to swear at and denigrate women – you will. If you believe you shouldn't hit a woman – you won't. If you believe women are inferior, you will speak and behave in ways that mirror your beliefs.

Sometimes digging out these values and beliefs is tricky. You may think you are a modern man but notice that when you are in relationship you have certain expectations that surprise you. I like cooking but I let my partner cook most of the meals, do the laundry and clean up the place – just like Mom did. *Very interesting!* It is our behavior that most gives us away. Look to your behavior to root out difficult to find values and beliefs. Feelings can also give you information. For example, what is your feeling when your wife asks you to do the dishes (or any activity that you have a reaction to)? Do you get angry, annoyed, put off, feel like she is nagging or trying to control you?

Skill Acquisition (part 1)

The ability to learn new skills is based on inherent or natural abilities, motivation and learning environment. As you are reading this book I will assume your motivation is high unless you were "forced" by a member of the opposite sex to make a change. In that case, as you are spending your time reading you might as well make the best of it and learn what you can. It's your time.

If you have the brain power to read you have the "talent" to understand and learn new behaviors. Acquiring new habits can be challenging not so much because of their inherent difficulty, but because you have to stop doing a deeply ingrained behavioral pattern – a habit. If you have ignored and not taken a woman's request with any seriousness for forty years you may be challenged to learn a new way of thinking, believing, and acting. On the other hand, I have seen instant change occur because the individual made a decision. Once made, the behaviors changed immediately and with no difficulty. It can happen. For most of us it will take some work . . . OK, a lot of work.

The learning environment in this case is a self-created environment with you in charge of how, when, and where you read the information and then what you do with it – to practice or not. Part of the environment is the home itself (assuming you are living with the other person) where you will practice with your partner. It is not so much the physical aspect but the interpersonal one that has a major influence on your learning. Getting support and buy-in from your significant other is important. She can help in your learning process. Indeed, if she is learning as well you can be mutually supportive.

Skill Acquisition (part 2)

Buddhists have a wonderful concept for learning new things. It is called, "beginner's mind." With all our knowledge and need as men to appear confident, competent, and in control, beginner's mind is not so easy. Beginner's mind is placing yourself in a mental state of not knowing anything about what you are learning. It is an emptying and opening up of your mind and consciousness. It is like being a child again. This can be uncomfortable as we often associate childhood with vulnerability and weakness. As an adult it is a highly efficient and a non-self-critical way of learning. Like a child learning to walk, he may fall thousands of times and yet the child never loses hope – he just keeps his eye on the objective – walking. And eventually you did learn to walk. You may have been frustrated a few times but you never stopped trying and you never ever said, "I can't do this" or "this is too hard." No, you just picked yourself off the floor and tried again.

Learning to communicate with women is the same if you can be in *beginner's mind*. When you are first learning you will make mistakes, feel emotions, and generally wish there was an easier way. There is. **Don't be in a relationship**! If however you want to be in a relationship, trust that over time your skills will improve and so will your relationships.

Warning: *It is still emotionally difficult for me when in a conflict with my partner. As many years as I have been practicing, it goes against my "guy"* *training and my personal issues with expressing anger with women to confront my partner. It is an effort each time. I have to take a big breath and dive in. The only reason I do is because of the results – a more satisfying relationship, feeling better about myself and . . . you guessed it, more sex!*

Life Practice

Practice will improve your ability to communicate with women. It will make it better and that is a lot – but it won't be perfect. It is hard to reach perfection when you are in communication with someone other than yourself. It can be complicated. Also, there is nothing worse than practicing something the wrong way. So, practice the right way:

- In your head
- Speaking out loud by yourself
- In front of a mirror (good for checking out your facial expressions)
- With someone other than whom the conversation is directed at if the subject matter is volatile
- And finally, with that special woman in your life.

In Chapters Ten and Eleven you will get a step-by-step process on how to set up and have a conversation.

Re-evaluation:

This is simply an evaluation of your efforts and then making the necessary changes to become even more effective. Evaluating your results is an ongoing process. The danger occurs when the relationship is going well and you get lazy or forgetful and stop checking on your partner. Or for that matter, sharing how you are doing.

Do you need to change? (Who says?)

Who says you should change? You, or someone close to you? If *you* say so, then it's a no-brainer. Start. If someone else says so . . . I suggest you stop, look and listen. While you stop, take a reading on your reaction. Were you pissed that she even suggested such a thing (big red sign, STOP and look at yourself) or were you surprised but interested or feeling relief that someone pointed out something you have always thought you should do?

If you are not sure just ask yourself if you:

- are satisfied in your relationship
- feel it could be better
- realize your partner is unhappy.

These are some questions to check out. Specifically, in the area of communication ask yourself:

- How do I fight? Is my communication full of swearing, put-downs and sarcastic retorts? If either one of you is into this kind of response it is imperative to STOP it immediately and move into respectful and responsible communication.
- Do you give commands?
- Do you ignore?
- Do you stonewall and withdraw?
- Do you fight like a lawyer trying to win every point?

If you do any one of the above you need to change if you want a successful relationship.

Be careful not to delude yourself if you happen to be an effective communicator at work whether with men or women. How you communicate with your significant other is a different proposition. We are vulnerable with those we care about the most. That is when the stakes are the highest and when our ego is at its most defensive.

If you are still not convinced go to the source and ask your partner. Listen to her response. Do not argue. If she says yes, then believe her. If you do not feel able to ask your partner, ask another female you are willing to trust. If you don't trust any woman I can assure you that you have a problem and not just with communication. Get professional help.

Why change?

Why change? Because, in the long run it is less painful and costly than not changing. In the beginning change can be painful and that is why so few people even attempt it. You on the other hand have the guts to be reading this book. You have admitted that something is not working (you may have known this for a long time) and have finally decided to create change.

Acknowledging there is a problem is step one, acquiring information and skills is step two (i.e., reading this book), and practice is step three. The cost of not changing is high. Ineffective communication skills with women results in troubled relationships (arguments, negative feelings, upset, reduction or elimination of sex – aaggghhh!) which leads to stress, which leads to unhappiness, and usually physical and emotional health problems. In worst case scenarios it leads to divorce. Divorce is expensive on all fronts – financial, emotional and physical.

Then there is the damage done to our children when we are in conflict with our partners whether we are divorced or still living together. The latest research clearly shows what the layperson always knew – divorce screws up our kids [36]. Children of divorce have higher rates of divorce than children from intact families, suffer higher rates of depression and anxiety, and have greater problems in school – especially boys. As hard as divorce is on the couple divorcing, it is even worse on the children. Does this mean I support staying together in all situations? Of course not! If there is physical or sexual violence on the spouse or children and an unwillingness or inability to change I would recommend leaving. In these situations it is often a choice between the lesser of two evils because most children, even in bad relationships, suffer when there is a divorce.

Benefits

Benefits of being able to communicate with women include:

- Fewer and shorter arguments
- Less emotional upset
- Less hurt feelings
- Feeling like you have a partner not an enemy
- More appreciation for and from your partner
- More interesting conversations
- Greater understanding of her and she of you
- Strengthening of the love bond
- Better able to manage the adversities of life
- Improved immune system
- Longer life (this is good)
- More and better sex.

As you learn to communicate you will notice that the whole family gains from your work. The level of self-esteem rises for you and your family. As you learn to listen, respect what your partner says and respond in a caring fashion, you are communicating powerfully. The message you send out is: I care, you are important and loveable. This leads your partner to feeling better about herself, thus improving her self-esteem. As her self-esteem improves she will naturally be more interesting and fun to be around. Assuming you are not threatened by this, your self-esteem will improve as well. It is a win-win situation of cascading benefits.

In a household of well-meaning people more effective decisions are made. The needs of both partners are heard and taken care of in mutually satisfying ways. Everyone loves attention and listening is the strongest message you send that shows and demonstrates attention. Intimacy increases as conflict is acknowledged openly and dealt with in a timely and responsible manner. This leads to a lessening of anxiety and fear in the household as conflict is normalized and not seen as a horrible event. As conflicts are resolved the relationship is strengthened. Furthermore, if you have children, they learn from you. They learn that conflict is natural and that it is possible to resolve conflict in non-hurtful ways. They learn that it is possible to be emotional and responsible at the same time. Amazing but true!

Strengths and learning (What works about you?)

Up to this point we have been looking at what needs to change or improve. Essentially, we are looking at weaknesses. Now we will look at your strengths. This is important for many reasons. One reason is that when you are in a relationship that is not working it is stressful and engenders a sense of incompetence, failure, lowered self-esteem and general unhappiness (unless it's all her fault. That was a joke, and if you believed it that is part of the problem). It takes two to tango, as the old saying goes, and it is important to take responsibility for your part of the problem. Often I work with guys who have no idea that they are contributing to the problem. They bring their wife into therapy and ask me to "fix her." More often than not he is the problem. But enough of weaknesses.

What works about you? What are your strengths? If you have been in a lousy relationship for a while it is easy to forget your good points. Your "bad" points have been screamed at you or quietly pointed out to you in no uncertain terms countless times and you are collapsing under this constant attack. Whether it is carpet bombing or smart bombs the result is the same – total destruction of self-worth.

If you have been blasted into numbness and can't remember when you had any positive traits, talk to your good friends and write. What I want you to do immediately is make a list of your positive traits or good qualities. Fill in the blanks below.

Examples include: I am humorous, open, honest, etc.

My Good Qualities

1) _____

2) _____

3) _____

4) _____

5) _____

If you have more than five attributes continue writing on the notes section or in your workbook.

What doesn't work about you?

Now that we have your good points list let's move on to the list that we all can easily fill. The list about what doesn't work. But before you begin, I want you to think first and only write down items that you know you could change if you wanted. For example, smoking, swearing less, not yelling all the time. That sort of thing. For some of you quitting smoking might seem like an impossibility – then don't put it down.

Behaviors I Want To Change

1) _____

2) _____

3) _____

4) _____

5) _____

Date: _____

Again, don't worry if you don't fill up the list, and if you have more to add use the note section at the back of the book. While you're at it, put a date on it. That way you can look at this list a month from now, three months from now, six months and a year later and see what you have accomplished.

Behavioral change: The road less traveled

Can you change your behavioral patterns – patterns that have been in place a lifetime? Yes. I have seen it time and time again. We can change. I have changed. You can change.

When we are confronted with failure in life it is often due to ineffective thinking and behavior. As guys we can be incredibly stubborn. "Why should I have to change?" is a refrain I commonly hear. The answer to such a question is simple. Keep doing the same old thing and you will keep getting the same old results. A definition of insanity is doing the same old thing over and over and expecting different results.

To change any habitual way of being is painful. That's why people don't change. It is easier to stay the same even when we are suffering. People will put up with absolutely horrible circumstances rather than change. It is the old devil you know rather than the devil you don't know. You know this pain. You know its parameters and can adjust. The problem is that it is killing you. And I am not speaking metaphorically. It really is making you unhealthy both psychologically and physically.

Changing an established way of thinking or behaving requires constant attention – tiring. It may give you a headache. It will definitely be tiring until it becomes a new habit. Notice how easy it is to: argue, shout, clam up, drink, or whatever it is you do that is not effective in your relationship. You know how to do that. Now, you will have to learn a new skill (or many).

Skill development: Practice, practice, practice

Yes, you have heard it time and time again. Practice makes perfect. I can assure you that in your relationship you will have countless opportunities to practice a new way of responding to your partner.

Tips:

1) Don't expect to do it perfectly all the time.

2) Practice becoming aware sooner and sooner when you feel yourself reacting.

3) It is never too late to apologize. Do it as soon as you realize what you have done. Obviously the sooner the better. It is also easier. The longer you wait the harder it becomes.

Video as verifier:

If you are having trouble identifying your difficulties I suggest being videoed. Video is stunning in its ability to wake you up. It is like a bucket of cold water being dumped over your head. Your wife can tell you ten thousand times that you stick your finger up your nose and you can deny it ten thousand times. But when you see it on video it is, "My God! I stick my finger up my nose. Why didn't you tell me? It's disgusting." Notice the shifting of blame to the wife for not telling him about his disgusting habit.

Admitting when we are wrong is a difficult thing for men to do. When caught in an undeniable truth about oneself the typical male will try to shift the uncomfortable spotlight to someone else. The best defense is a good offense and so we use denial or blame or misdirection to exonerate the behavior.

How could one use denial even with a video. Easy! "That's not me. It just looks like me." This would of course be difficult to do in the household but not impossible. Just this week I was visiting relatives and there was a conversation about the Great Wall of China while watching the Olympics. The wife, of one of my relatives, said she thought it was 4,000 miles long. The husband started arguing saying it could not possibly be longer than 1,700 miles. I suggested we look it up on Wikipedia. Sure enough, the Wall is 4,000 miles long. The husband then said, and I kid you not, "But she didn't know it was 4,000 miles, she just *thought* it was." As if the wife's saying what she thought the length of the wall was, was not the same as knowing and therefore she was wrong.

This kind of logic is used by men when arguing with women because they (men) cannot stand to lose, and especially lose to women, and especially about something involving facts. You see, men use their knowledge about facts and world events to help them stay in a one-up position. Unfortunately, it is a useless and destructive behavior with intimate relationships.

Blind spots:

Blind spots are tricky. We can't see them. It is hard to believe someone when they say something that you don't believe. They must be crazy. Well, maybe not. If a car is in your blind spot, just because you can't see it doesn't mean it's not there. Likewise, if your partner says something about you that you cannot see, it might be in your best interest to at least consider it before you have an avoidable accident. This takes trust. Whoa! Do you even want to go there? Do you trust your partner? If you don't, this is indicative of the state of your relationship – not good.

Practicalities of Video:

There are a number of ways to use the video. You could set it up on a tripod in the most commonly used room and turn it on. You can set it up when having a scheduled meeting; like a talk about how to parent, or a house meeting with the whole family, or a talk on vacation planning or, a guaranteed winner – talk about money. This will make for fun and informative viewing. Maybe not fun at the time but definitely informative.

When viewing the video have the controller in hand so that you can stop and talk about what just happened, play something over again and take the time to analyze what is happening. When were you OK? What plugged you in? What was your body language? Where did the conversation go off the rails and why?

Making a decision

If you bought this book that was your first decision action for change. If someone else bought it for you then reading it was your first step for change. But maybe the first decision came even before that when you said to yourself, "Something has to change." And lo and behold, this book appeared on your doorstep. The Universe works in mysterious ways. The next important decision is to commit to change. To commit to having a better relationship. To commit to learning how to communicate effectively. And, to commit to doing whatever is necessary to bring about the needed changes. Are you committed? Yes. Great! Now you are ready to create an action plan to bring about the changes that will lead to learning how to communicate with women.

Creating a plan:

This is real simple. There are only seven steps that will lead to more effective communication between you and your partner. Here they are.

Step 1: Read the book

Step 2: Fill out all the lists (make your life easy and do it while reading)

Step 3: Create your Action Plan

Step 4: Talk with your spouse about what you are going to do

Step 5: Start implementing the steps from the Action Plan

Step 6: Review, Analyze and Revamp

Step 7: Repeat until desired results are achieved

Success may sound easy but doing it requires courage, ongoing commitment and persistence in carrying out the action plan. I guarantee that it will be emotional at times (this is where the courage comes in), frustrating at times (this is where the persistence comes in) and you will want to throw in the towel at times (this is where your commitment comes in) but if you work through it all, you will be rewarded.

Learning new habits and breaking life-long ineffective habits takes effort. You will have to become aware of unconscious thoughts and actions. You will be challenging yourself on a daily basis and, like working out at the gym, you will get sore. There will be the temptation to go back to your old and familiar ways of thinking and behaving – don't. And if you do, get back on the wagon as soon as possible. Always keep your goals foremost in your mind's eye – learning effective communication which leads to a better relationship and more sex.

This is not a journey for wimps. On the up side, the rewards are high. In fact, they are the best rewards that life has to offer and you would be crazy not to go for it. So what are you waiting for?

Summary:

The Pyramid of Change consists of five steps. They are problem recognition, motivation to change, examining attitudes, values and beliefs, skill acquisition, practicing the new skill sets and change. There is a sixth step and that is evaluating the effectiveness of your implementation and making changes as necessary and then practice the revamped model.

Before beginning the change process it is important to honestly examine whether or not you need and want to change. If your relationship is not working that may be a clue that something needs to change. But, do you want to change? Change is time consuming and takes effort. Also, maybe you're not the problem. At the very least you know you have a problem which means something has to change if you want change in your life.

There are many advantages to changing the way you communicate with your partner. In the long run you will be happier, healthier and live longer. In the short run you will have fewer arguments, upset, hurt feelings and more sex. Over time you will feel like you have a supportive partnership with your spouse. Conversations will be more interesting, you will manage the stresses and strains of life better and there will be harmony in the household.

On the personal side, your self-esteem will rise, you will feel more confident, and because you are having fewer arguments and getting more sex you will be more relaxed and happier.

Realizing and identifying your strengths is important if you want to improve self-esteem. By identifying your strengths you also give yourself encouragement to tackle the areas that you want to change. Behavioral change is a road few are willing to engage with as it involves changing long held habits (takes effort) and can often bring up emotions (what men fear most).

In this chapter you identified your strengths and areas you wanted to improve on. Now it is a matter of practice. You will have plenty of opportunities and if you are having a difficult time seeing your blind spots using video can be helpful.

Because you want to use the most effective approach to accomplish your goals, creating a plan is essential.

This part of the process is so important I am going to repeat it:

Step 1: Read the book

Step 2: Fill out all the lists (make your life easy and do it while reading)

Step 3: Create your Action Plan

Step 4: Talk with your spouse about what you are going to do

Step 5: Start implementing the steps from the Action Plan

Step 6: Review, Analyze and Revamp

Step 7: Repeat until desired results are achieved

Chapter 5

THE ACTION PLAN

Planning without action is futile,
action without planning is fatal.

Anon

Why a plan?

The Great Pyramids, the Eiffel Tower and the Empire State Buildings all used plans. A relationship is even more complex yet no one has a plan. And we wonder why the divorce rate is 50% in the USA and 37% in Canada and half of the other 50% can't stand their partners (my guesstimate). In a recent poll [37] of 207 women, 40% labeled their biggest frustration of their married lives was that their husbands "didn't communicate enough." If the foundation is shaky, like the story of the Three Little Pigs, when an adversarial situation comes knocking at your door, it will huff and puff and blow your relationship down. So build with brick and mortar and learn to communicate.

Having a plan accomplishes many things including:

- Having a specific aim or purpose. Gives you a direction. It's nice to know where you're going.
- Feeling more secure for taking action and not just having an

idea in your head.

- Accountability. You get to see where you are, where you've come from, and where you are going. This helps to create strategies for measuring the effectiveness of your actions.
- Gives you something to show her when things are a little rough – demonstrating that you do indeed – "Have a plan."

Commitment

But are you committed? And I don't mean in a small way, but in a HUGE way. This is your present and possibly future relationships we are talking about. Being in a healthy relationship has benefits both physical and psychological. It is worth your time and effort to make these changes so that you will have a happier household, feel better about yourself and get more and better sex. Can I be any clearer than that? Because,

Until one is committed, there is hesitancy, the chance to draw back. Concerning all acts of initiative (and creation), there is one elementary truth, the ignorance of which kills countless ideas and splendid plans: that the moment one definitely commits oneself, then Providence moves too. All sorts of things occur to help one that would never otherwise have occurred. A whole stream of events issues from the decision, raising in one's favor all manner of unforeseen incidents and meetings and material assistance, which no man could have dreamed would have come his way. Whatever you can do, or dream you can do, begin it. Boldness has genius, power, and magic in it. Begin it now.

William Hutchinson Murray (1913-1996), from his 1951 book *The Scottish Himalayan Expedition.*

When one is committed the world does indeed move in mysterious ways. Another saying that supports this concept is – the world gets out of the way for someone who knows where he is going. Creating a plan helps you clarify where you are going and acts as a reference so that you are reminded of the steps to take, when to take them and to what end. To get to the end you have to have a beginning. So, let's start.

Start Date

The best plans have a start date. Yours should be now. I recommend that you sign your commitment to having a better relationship by learning and practicing effective communication skills:

I, _____ , (print name) commit to improving my relationship(s) by learning and practicing effective communication skills starting today.

_____   _____
(signature)   (date)

Congratulations! This is your second commitment. Your first was buying and or reading this book. By signing your name you have put pen to paper and made a declaration to the universe. The universe is always listening. By completing this step you have made concrete that which was simply an intangible desire.

My experience is that when you commit, the universe invariably says, "really," and proceeds to test just how committed you are. So don't be surprised at how quickly and intensely you are tested. You have just begun to read this book and you may be laughed at, scorned, and ridiculed. "You're a guy. There's no way you will change. What do you know about communication?" This attack may come from male friends who want to keep you in line because if you change they know their wives will be after them to change. Or it may come from your partner, who doesn't want to get her hopes up and then have them dashed (or she may have to change herself as the result of your changes).

However, you have been warned and you are now fore-armed. You will not let petty minds distract you from the holy grail of your mission – to learn how to communicate with women! This is your vision. Now, let's get started by first identifying our goals.

Goals

What are your goals in this relationship? I am assuming that you have some idea of what you want. Saying you want a better relationship is too vague. It is important to get specific. I want to communicate better. That is better but an important aspect of goal setting is the ability to measure what it is you want. If we can't measure it, it is harder to determine if the improvement is real or imaginary. Therefore, what does better communication look like? "We would be able to talk without screaming at each other." This is measureable! "Currently we scream at each other 100% of the time we talk. If our communication improves, this number will decrease. Hey, now we only scream 50% of the time. This is a big improvement." To be most effective goals should be:

1. Written
2. Specific
3. Measureable
4. Achievable

Written: Putting your ideas into the written form is a magical process. First, it demands that you be clear as to what you want. Vagueness coalesces into clarity. Your target now becomes clear and in the process your mind becomes focused. Second, you have a record of your thoughts. You can't forget (unless you misplace it) what you want. Third, you can relax knowing that you don't have to be constantly trying to remember what it is. Just go look it up. Finally, writing it down makes what you want more concrete to yourself and to the universe. It is a step forward from idea to concrete reality.

Specific: The universe loves clarity and specificity. As in William Murray's quote, when one is committed the universe wants to support you, however, if you are vague, you will get lots of vague support. Be specific. Not, I want more sex. I want sex once a week, twice a week, three times a week – whatever it is – be specific. Otherwise you will just end up masturbating more often.

Measureable: Measureable is something you can count. This is simple. Like the example above, when I ask for sex three times a week I can easily measure if I hit my goal or not. If I say I want to cut down our fighting from four times a week to once a week I can measure it. If I say I want to fight less often, how do you really know? Some weeks might feel less and at other times it might feel like more depending on how bad the fights were, how you felt about yourself, and a whole host of factors that contribute to your assessment. We want something measureable. When you measure, it forces you to focus and be accountable. Who knows, maybe you only fight once a week but you thought or felt like it was three times. What does this mean? Maybe things are not as bad as you thought.

Or, maybe you don't like conflict. Or maybe, you want to only fight once a month. Measureable!

Achievable: "I never want another argument with my wife for as long as I live." Nice idea but you will be sorely disappointed if this is your goal. It is important that you start small with a goal that is winnable and then move up to bigger goals as you build up your confidence and abilities. This is so important when you are starting out as the habits in the relationship are strongly ingrained and will resist change. Winning is a much better feeling than losing – again. Start racking up those wins and you and your partner will get excited about the positive change that is occurring and this will feed into an ever increasing cycle of faster and bigger changes.

K.I.S.S.: Keep it simple stupid. Notice I haven't softened the blow. Keep it simple silly and other changes to this acronym make me want to barf. Life is unfair, bad things happen to good people and I get to see what happens when people do not address the obvious. Sometimes we do stupid things. I do, you do and so does everybody else. Own up to it and move on.

K.I.S.S. as applied to goals is . . . simple. Pick three. Make them short. Make it specific, measureable and achievable. Here is an example and space for you to write your goals:

Goal #1: Not walk away from my wife when she is angry at least 3 times this week (we argue every day).

Goal # 2: To have a unified front when it comes to disciplining the kids (what does this mean in measurable terms? Talk this out with your partner, get clear and then make a log of how you are doing).

Goal # 3: To make love at least twice a week.

Note: *You must have control over the goals. In example #3 above you need your partner's agreement to make out twice this week. If she agrees – fine. To be more controllable, the goal should be stated as "I will request or initiate love-making twice this week." Asking, requesting or initiating is in your control. Her agreement is not in your control.*

Your turn:

Goal # 1: _____

Goal # 2: _____

Goal # 3: _____

The "S" word

S is for support. Even writing this word takes my breath away. Support! What a concept. I have been brought up to do it all by myself. If I need help, especially on personal issues, I am being weak and certainly not being a strong man. Most men only even consider support when their wife threatens a divorce (and means it) and insists on going to marriage counseling. Yuck, how embarrassing. How demeaning, how . . . childish not to be able to admit there is a problem, admit that you haven't been able to solve it, and admit that you need help. Our ego is not our friend in these situations.

When you realize that your relationship is causing you stress it is important to admit this ASAP. Otherwise you will do some incredibly stupid things like: getting an ulcer, becoming violent or having an affair. Here is a cautionary tale that I would like you to consider:

One day long ago when I was young, in shape, and a handsome dude, I met a very attractive woman. She smiled, laughed at my jokes and was willing to go to bed with me. I was in heaven. Two weeks into this budding relationship an incident happened. We had gone to a fast food outlet. I went inside to buy our hamburger and fries while she waited in the car. I returned to the car, gave her the food and started eating. Apparently something was either wrong with the food or I did something that she did not like. Before I knew it, food was flying in the air. Ketchup was all over the place. It was on my windshield, on the seats, on my clothes. I was dumbstruck. I have never been the victim of a woman's anger/violence nor did I see this in my family. I started to cry. I am not an easy person to make cry and yet I started crying. I must have thought that this behavior meant the relationship was over. I was not so lucky. I thought that this was outrageous behavior but I was needy for love. Even though this was only week two of the relationship, I was deep into it. How deep? Very deep apparently. I stayed on for three years of misery. By the second year I had an ulcer. Even this was not enough to make me leave. I knew things were bad but I did not know what to do about it. I did not know where to turn for support. I did not know about counseling or marriage therapy. So I floundered around like a dying fish on the deck of a boat gasping for air, dazed and confused.

This is a sad tale of someone (me) who had no support systems in place when it came to dealing with interpersonal relationships. This was trial and error at its worst. I don't recommend it. Unfortunately, I see it all the time in my practice.

There are many types of support. As I got older I started to use my friends, I took workshops, and I went to couple's counseling. This was wonderful. In the counseling my belief that I wasn't misreading the relationship was affirmed. Getting an unbiased third party opinion is a valuable process. Even if you see that you have some areas that need to be worked on. Now you know you can apply yourself if you choose.

At one point I joined a men's group. That was inspiring and I highly recommend it. A men's group gives you the opportunity to discuss issues in a supportive atmosphere. They can support you to get what you want, share their successes and failures and make you feel "normal." In this supportive environment you get to examine questions about life, yourself, and anything else that happens to be of concern.

There are formal areas of support that you can tap into. It could be your religious organization or the spiritual leader of that organization in your community. Another free space is the community mental health clinics. They often have programs for individuals and groups. This could be individual psychotherapy or group counseling for specific issues like anger management, depression, and anxiety to name a few. If drugs or drinking are problematic there is AA and NA. Community Centers often have relevant programs for low cost.

Moving up the ladder (money wise) there is individual and group therapy offered by private practitioners. Most men are hesitant when they consider going to therapy. You will have to swallow your ego and admit you are having difficulty. You do not have to be sick to see a therapist! On the contrary. Therapy can offer another perspective, it can be someone to bounce ideas off of, it can be an opportunity to vent your frustrations, get support, get information, and formulate an action plan. Therapy can be all this and more.

Log book: 21 days to a new habit

Dr. Maltz, in *Psychocybernetics* [38], first put forth the idea that 21 days was needed to train our mind to a new habit. The corollary of this statement is that you have to not do something for 21 days to extinguish a habit. What I have found works best in my practice is to do both together. Stop doing your bad habit and replace it with a new healthy one. This is an important concept. We do our habits for a reason. Just because you stop it doesn't mean whatever need it fulfilled goes away. For example, someone stops smoking and starts gambling. You stop eating chocolate cake and start eating apple pie with ice cream. You get the idea. The trick is to replace the unhealthy habit with a healthy one. Instead of pacing and chewing your nails when anxious – you go for a run. Instead of smoking cigarettes to calm your anxiety – you meditate. Your turn.

<u>Habits To Change</u>

Habit to Drop	Replacement	Start Date
X. Eating chocolate bars	Eat fresh fruit	Oct 12, 20XX
1. _____	_____	_____
2. _____	_____	_____
3. _____	_____	_____

Buy-in from partner

Plans are great but, for the highest odds of success, it is critical to get buy-in from your partner. There are at least three reasons for this:

1) She can help you when you forget or are unaware of what you are doing (e.g., you are shouting at the kids and just did not realize how loud you were)
2) as a feedback mechanism your partner can tell you how you are doing (e.g., practicing paraphrasing or any other communication skill)
3) for encouragement.

By telling your partner what you are up to she will feel involved in the process and see that there is a plan in place for change. This will encourage her and give her hope for the future. It is at this stage of sharing with her that any impracticalities in the idea can be worked out. For example, you want to do your workouts on Monday, Wednesday, and Friday morning at 7 a.m. and she points out that on Wednesday mornings you have a meeting with your parole officer, prayer group, or business network. "Ah, thanks honey for reminding me." She smiles at you and feels good for being helpful and being recognized. You are happy for avoiding a double booking.

Practice makes perfect (maybe not perfect, but it should improve things)

If you want to learn to communicate effectively with your wife you will have to practice. Like anything in life, skill is attained through repetition. All the great talents in sports and music practice and practice a lot.

So don't get down if after the second attempt at a new skill it is not perfect – it won't be. This is where patience will be required and remember buy-in. Your partner will need patience as well. But as long as you are making the effort and slowly but surely making progress your efforts will not be in vain.

What you can do after an interaction is the After Argument Analysis™ or what I call the 3A. It is simple and works like this. After you have experienced the completion of an argument or discussion and the emotions have settled down, grab a pen and some paper. If your partner is up for it do this together. Put the date on the paper, what the argument was about, how long it lasted and analyze what happened including what worked and what did not. It might look something like this:

Saturday June 8, 20XX
2 – 4 p.m.

Had an argument about what she bought when we went to Wal-Mart. I was angry that she spent two hundred dollars on clothes when she has a closet full of clothes. I started screaming at her as soon as the kids went out to play. She started crying and said I'm always yelling at her and besides, it's her money and she needs new clothes for the fall season. I stopped yelling (said I was sorry for yelling) and said that I don't understand why she needs clothes for the fall – what's wrong with last year's clothes. I wear the same clothes. She said I look like a slob. I said I always look this way. She said, "Yeah, it's disgusting, I feel ashamed to be walking with you." This went on for about an hour and a half, her crying, me getting angry, hurling insults back and forth. Finally, I said, "Look, I get that as a woman in your job (a paralegal) you have to look half decent and it is your money. I see my paycheck and your paycheck as our money. Maybe we need to discuss, before we go shopping, what we are going to buy. In truth, I get freaked out that we won't have enough money to pay the mortgage and all the bills." When I mentioned my feelings she was surprised to hear that I was worried. She said that she was worried too and thought that I just didn't care. We were able to discuss things in a calm way after this point. At the end we hugged and she said she loved me even if I dressed poorly and how about we go shopping next week for some clothes for me. I said I felt uncomfortable about this but let's talk about it before we go shopping.

Then list what worked and what didn't. Keep this in your log book.

Day-to-day and week-to-week

Make entries whenever you are involved in a communication with a member of the opposite sex. This is important as over time you may start to see patterns that will help you understand contributing factors to ineffective communication. You might notice that you always have arguments right before meal times. Maybe you suffer from hypoglycemia and you are at your most irritable just before eating. If this were so you can take preventative action – a snack or not engaging in any touchy topics until after eating. This info would be useful for your spouse as well. This is a simple example that is easily rectified (this is true of my spouse. I have learned not to even try to engage in conversation when she is hungry).

Maybe it is the topics that are upsetting. You notice that most of your arguments are about the kids. If this is true, you don't need to waste time on other issues but can focus on how to deal with the kids.

Responsibility through reporting

By keeping an ongoing log you will be starting to gain control over the situation by:

1) feeling like you are taking action (we guys like action)

2) amassing data (something concrete)

3) being able to analyze and understand the who, what, when and where of the problem.

With this information you can become more aware and take preemptive action to reduce the stress and become more effective. The by-product is increased self-confidence and improved relationships.

Setting new goals

As you begin to score, success in communication that is, you can start raising the bar. In other words, looking at the more difficult or subtle areas that are getting in the way of great communication skills with your partner. Once again, communicate with your partner where you think you have improved and to what degree, to see if you have agreement. If yes, great! If no, examine where she thinks you still need to improve and maybe even how (she might have some good ideas).

Work with your partner to establish the next most important area to work on. It is best to work on one aspect at a time otherwise it can be overwhelming. That being said, it is good to know the overall skills and processes involved. They are the map that show you the territory and the specific item you are focusing on is the daily road trip you embark on to get from A (where you are) to B (where you want to be).

Coping with bad days

Like any voyage there will be some bad days. A sudden squall will come out of nowhere to blindside you. You may hit a pothole or a rock on the road, blow a tire, or run out of gas (literally and figuratively). In the beginning it will be two steps forward and half a dozen backwards. Your partner will become exasperated and you will question her lack of patience and your self-esteem may take a battering.

Like a wise sailor in a storm, head for safety! This may mean taking some time away on a fishing trip, an evening bowling with the guys or going on a silent retreat with some monks. Whatever works for you, just don't ignore the warning signs. It takes energy to change yourself and time to recharge the batteries when you are emotionally exhausted.

When you come back to the arena tell your partner that you are committed to your final destination and ready to set sail again. Check in to see how she is doing. Are her sails tattered and hanging limply from the masts? If so, suggest that she take some time off for repairs.

Summary:

Having a plan dramatically increases the odds of achieving your goals. The plan gives you direction, an end point and is a reference should you get lost. Essentially, it is a map for your journey. And, like any difficult journey, you need to be committed.

To strengthen a commitment it is helpful to write it down, date it and sign it. This makes it real. Takes it from just an idea and starts to make it a reality. Likewise, your goals should be written, specific, measurable and achievable. Goals should also be simple. Apply the K.I.S.S. concept when in doubt.

As in any large undertaking having support is essential to improve the odds of success. This may require letting go of old beliefs like, *I should be able to do this on my own if I was a real man, only sissies need help, and it is weak to have to ask for help.* You have friends for a reason. Now is the time to use them. If you don't have friends look to your relatives. No luck there . . . then find a support group. If you can't find a support group find a therapist or a relationship coach. If you can't find one go to my website www. therelationshipguy.ca and get connected.

Remember change doesn't happen overnight. You may have a list of behaviors to change so don't overwhelm yourself. Take one step – one behavior at a time. Get success and build upon it.

Getting buy-in from your partner, even though not absolutely necessary, will help make the whole process easier and quicker. Either way, seeing is believing and if you start to change and maintain your change she will have no option but to acknowledge this and respond accordingly. If she doesn't, then you have some hard decisions to make.

After that, it is practice until the new ways of thinking and behaving are automatic. Keeping a journal or log book can be helpful in the process. It provides a written record of the process from which patterns can be identified, it feels like you are doing something, helps clarify events, and makes sense of your experience.

Chapter 6

WHAT DOES YOUR PARTNER WANT?

Whether they give or refuse,
it delights women just the same to have been asked.

Ovid

They want the whole bloody world it seems. At times it certainly feels like that but it is an exaggeration. When we feel the demands for time, attention, certain behaviors and personality changes – it can be overwhelming. Fortunately, the reality is not as bad or as large as our fears. Below is a passage taken from an email, with permission, by a woman addressing what she wants from a man:

I think it is always the best to be honest with the other person, at all costs and above all. This has not always happened to me and I believe that no good can come of any relationship if both parties involved are not honest with each other . . . . What it all comes down to it at the end of the day, women just want to feel safe and valued and important in her man's life. He doesn't HAVE to feel like the "white knight in shining armor." Most of us just want that hug or a kiss at the end of the day. The world's problems do not have to be solved – we just need someone there who cares about us. It's not rocket science really. We all (women and males alike) make the mistake of MAKING ASSUMP-TIONS. Do not be scared to be courageous enough to ask questions. Life IS risky business but if we all just sit on the fence and DO NOT take risks, are we really living then??? I think we all know the answer to that. Love (for women) will always come first – just be willing to accept the precious gift of love that a woman might be giving you or you might miss out on something truly special and remarkable. You just have to meet it all half way and take the leap. . . .

Dr. Steve: Take care for now and thanks for your listening ear and advice – I've thought about it a lot.

Sincerely,
Carmin

To sum up, Carmin says that she wants:

- Honesty
- To feel safe, valued and important to her man
- A hug and a kiss at the end of the day
- Someone to care about her
- Acceptance of her love
- You to take some risks
- You to meet her half-way
- You to be able to ask questions.

She also has some suggestions for what **not** to do:

- Don't feel like you have to solve all the world's problems
- Be careful about making ASSUMPTIONS
- You don't have to be the knight in shining armor.

Even though this is only one woman's point of view, I find it consistent with what I hear in therapy. There are other items that women want generally and specifically. Each woman is unique in her needs and wants. The most common themes I hear revolve around being heard and respected.

Ask and ye shall receive

Every woman is different. Yes, I know, they share many similar qualities but what works for one will not necessarily work for another. As Carmin said, watch the assumptions. The best way to find out what she wants is to ask. How tough can this be? Listen and record what she says. I keep this list on my wall at my desk. Whenever I sense that I should be doing something for the relationship but not sure what, I just look at *The List* and pick something. I also make a note (check mark) of what I pick so that I don't pick the same thing every time. You do not want to be boring to your partner.

I cannot overemphasize the importance of The List. There are some things to know when creating The List. First, don't argue as she is telling you what she wants or likes to do with you. Saying "but I do that all the time" will not win you brownie points and will derail the process quickly. However, do ask questions for clarity. If she says I want flowers, and you're thinking, *I buy her flowers every month*, ask, "How often would you like flowers, honey?" To this she may say, "Every week dear." Ah-ha, now you know. It doesn't matter if you think this is unnecessary and once a month should suffice. This is what she wants. You have discovered an incredibly valuable piece of information. Write it down.

Second, when told a concept – ask for specifics. If she says, "I want security," or "intimacy," or to "feel loved," find out *exactly* what this means. This may take some time. She may not know. The *feeling* has to be translated into concrete tangible items you can manifest so that when she is feeling the need for security, you know exactly what you can do to support her (e.g., listen, buy her chocolates, hold her hand – whatever she has told you).

In effect you are creating two lists. One, which has a list of items that your partner likes to do or receive, and another, which tells you what to do or how to behave in given situations (e.g., when I'm upset do this).

It will be critical that when you are hearing what she wants concerning your behavior that you don't react. This is easier said than done. Learn to take a big breath and go for clarity. Don't try to prove her wrong when she says you're "insensitive." If you are surprised (and even if you're not), ask how this looks. In other words, "what do I do or say when I'm being insensitive?" Write this down and then ask what she would prefer or what would work for her. If I haven't mentioned it already, you're going to need a notebook to write all this stuff in.

Remember, you may not always agree with how she thinks you are – so what! This is *her* perception. Your job is to be like the archeologist and dig deep and with great care to understand what is before you. It is to your advantage to understand her perceptions and what she needs. Then and only then will you be at a point where you can make intelligent decisions on whether or not you are willing to do as requested. Otherwise, you are flailing around in the dark not knowing how to appease this insatiable monster.

What Makes Her Happy

Examples: Go out for walks, go to the movies, flowers, restaurant once a week, etc.

1) _____

2) _____

3) _____

4) _____

5) _____

6) _____

7) _____

8) _____

9) _____

10) _____

Once you have The List post it. Post it somewhere that you will see it on a daily basis. Also, add to it as you become aware of new items.

I cannot overemphasize how important these lists are. As I have said before, the above list is posted on my wall in front of the computer and it has saved my ass on more than one occasion.

What To Do When She Is Upset

Examples: Listen, hold her hand, stand still and look at her, turn off the TV, etc.

1) _____

2) _____

3) _____

4) _____

5) _____

6) _____

7) _____

8) _____

9) _____

10) _____

Don't argue - just listen

I've said it before and I'll say it again, just listen. You don't have to argue. The point is not to be right, to tell her where she is wrong, or to inform her. The point is to listen and be able to "get" what she is thinking and feeling. To get what her thoughts are on the subject and be able to communicate back to her what she said. Our instinct is to solve, correct, adjust, modify and be right. We want to find the correct, the best, and the most efficient solution. Well, I'll tell you what it is. LISTEN. That's it. Keep your mouth shut and your ears and mind open. Listen and remember and then repeat what you heard. If you can't repeat it accurately ask her to say it again until you are able to repeat it back accurately. When you get good at this you will be able to identify the content and the tone or emotional aspect of her experience without providing a solution – this is called paraphrasing.

Ask questions – get clear

Ask questions until you get it. Asking questions tells your partner that you are listening and care enough to stay present. It also focuses you on what she is saying instead of your answers to her plight. Asking questions helps you to avoid the minefield of a good answer that she doesn't need or want. What does she want? Ask. What does she need? Ask. What does she like? Ask. How can you help? Ask questions and listen.

Tip: *When asking questions don't sound like a lawyer grilling the opposition. Be gentle and inquisitive.*

Separate her perception from yours

Men and women often have two different experiences of the same event. You do not have to change her experience – unless you want a fight. It's OK that she sees it differently than you. I know this is hard to understand but if you insist that your reality is the right reality you will have difficulty in relationships and your communications until the day you die.

Instead of immediately rolling your eyes in disbelief at what she has just said, pause and take a breath. Tell yourself, this is interesting and I don't have to change her mind. Then ask a question to elicit understanding of how she came to believe what she does or how she is experiencing the event. Try not to sound like a royal inquisitor. She will get defensive.

Note differences

As you ask open-ended-questions (questions requiring more than just a yes or no answer) start to keep track of the differences between how she sees the issue and how you see it. During this process she will probably sense that you have a different experience and will inquire about it. This is great as it is an opportunity for you to share your reality. Out of this dialogue you may come to a new and more complex understanding of what happened or see that there is more than one way of interpreting the same event. Either way you will have had an interesting talk with your partner rather than a fight. Which do you prefer?

Dig deeper – go for understanding

In male to female conversations the facts are just the surface elements. To be more effective in your communication and relationship dig deeper and look for understanding. A good way to accomplish this is to ask questions about the emotional content. First, get the facts, and then the emotions. As you understand the emotions involved you will start to realize the complexity of her experience. The next layer is the relationships that exist between her and the event, which means people. Who is involved and what are the dynamics between them both historically and during the event. This is where guys tend to get lost big time. Research [39] shows that relationships are extremely important for women and their sexual functioning. We take a much simpler approach – we don't think about relationships too much. They are either working or not. If they are working great, and if not – too bad.

This is not how women operate around relationships. The psychological explanations, what women have told me, and my experience, is that women's lives revolve around relationships (men's around accomplishing things) and therefore they are much more attuned to all the subtle energies flowing between people. So, when she starts talking about how Aunt Suzie was upset by not receiving a compliment from your sister about the decorations at Grandma Beth's 80th Birthday party and you're thinking – you got to be joking – keep that as a thought and say something like, "Really, I hadn't noticed (which is true), tell me more." She will tell you more (guaranteed).

At some point after you have all the relevant facts, emotions involved, and the inter-relationships, then ask how this affects her. She may feel guilty or angry or fed up with how family members hold grudges – whatever. But now you have gotten to the nub of the issue and you can either bore deeper (or be more deeply bored) if you think this is what she wants or nod your head empathetically and say, "I see why you feel this way." Bingo! Bonus points are coming your way buddy! You didn't say something like "that is the most ridiculous thing I've ever heard," or "what difference does it make," or "is that all you women do – gossip." No. You listened, asked questions, supported her to express herself and discover complex relationships and then *validated her experience*. You are more than good and will be rewarded tonight.

The List

You may have an idea of what she wants or you may not. Either way, to gain clarity it is important to have a conversation with your partner and ask. And like all successful business meetings, notes should be taken or in this case, create a list. There are two parts to this section. The first list is "what she wants in a relationship." The second list is her "what she doesn't want list."

Example: 1. Feel like I am loved. Ask for details. What does this look like? For example, "I want you to tell me once a week that you love me, buy me flowers once a week and hug me every day." It is critical that you have the concrete or doable and measurable elements of any concept she brings up.

<u>What She Wants In A Relationship</u>

This is similar to the "what makes her happy list."

1) _____

2) _____

3) _____

4) _____

5) _____

6) _____

7) _____

8) _____

9) _____

10) _____

Now, create the – What she Doesn't Want list

<u>What She Doesn't Want</u>

1) _____

2) _____

3) _____

4) _____

5) _____

6) _____

7) _____

8) _____

9) _____

10) _____

Summary:

Even though it seems that women are never satisfied with us and want the whole world, in reality, they want just a few basic things. They want to be accepted, loved, and to feel safe and valued. They want a hug and a kiss at the end of the day. They want someone who treats them with respect and listens to what they have to say.

If you are confused as to what women want then ASK. As Carmin said, please don't make assumptions. Making a List of what your partner wants and likes will help you remember, especially when tired or irritable. Also, remember to go for specificity. General concepts mean little without concrete and actionable tasks.

To attain a high level of clarity with your spouse it is imperative that you listen, don't argue, let her have her experience, do not offer solutions, ask open-ended questions (questions that cannot be answered by a yes or no) and go beyond the facts to understanding her emotions and relationships, and finally, validating her experience.

Chapter 7

WHAT DO YOU WANT?

Without the transcendent and the transpersonal, we get sick . . . or else
hopeless and apathetic. We need something bigger that we are to be awed
by and to commit ourselves to.

Abraham Maslow

What do you want? This is an important question to ask. If you see yourself as needing to do all the changing and focusing exclusively on your partner's needs you will become resentful or emasculated or both. Remember, women want you to be a man not a mouse. You have needs. They are the usual ones. Sex is pretty high on the list but so are love, security, appreciation, and many other items. Before we get into the top ten list of what you want, here are some things to think about.

What to think about when creating your list

First, close your eyes and take a deep breath. Ask yourself what are the most important things you want out of your relationship. When something pops into your head write it down. Don't worry if you can't think of ten things. After you have your items written down, look to see if there is a need for clarification. For example, if you wrote sex, ask yourself how often. You want it every day. Your partner might want it once a month. What is your bottom line? Once a week, twice a week, every day? This is critical to identify. If you and your partner cannot agree or come up with a work around (e.g., a mistress – very popular in Europe, masturbation, or your blow-up doll – however, the solution must be acceptable to both partners) the relationship may not work.

Second, look at what you have put down and examine if it is really important or just a whimsy. Is it really important that she be willing to do a pole dance for you? It might be nice, but it certainly will not make or break the relationship. On the other hand, having her stop putting you down in public may be extremely important to you.

Third, when writing down a negative, like the example just given, also write the positive version of what you want. For example, I want to be given praise or appreciated – what would this look like, in what areas, how?

We now have two lists to create: 1) What I Want In A Relationship and, 2) What I Don't Want In A Relationship. Here's an example:

1) Sex twice a week, once during the week and once on the week-end.

What I Want In A Relationship

1) _____

2) _____

3) _____

4) _____

5) _____

6) _____

7) _____

8) _____

9) _____

10) _____

Now, create the – What I Don't Want In A Relationship list.

What I Don't Want In A Relationship

Example: 1.   To be put down in front of our friends.

1) _____

2) _____

3) _____

4) _____

5) _____

6) _____

7) _____

8) _____

9) _____

10) _____

No arguments

If you put down that you wanted no arguments on your list, I advise you to make a change because *it's not going to happen.* If by some chance you are currently in a relationship in which no arguments occur – look out! This is almost a sure sign that one or both of the partners do not know how to express themselves. I have had a number of clients come to me and state that they don't argue. I feel like asking them, "Then why are you getting a divorce?" They still don't get it.

Arguing is a normal and healthy thing to do. How you argue is critical. If you are nasty, use profane language and belittle your partner you will end up with an unhappy relationship. If on the other hand you are respectful, expressive, responsible for your feelings and willing to listen to the other side, you will have a happier relationship and more sex. Remember, unhappy women do not want to make love. Now, you may want to put down that you want to argue less and have arguments that actually resolve a problem or lead to better understanding.

The Serenity Prayer

I love the Serenity prayer:

> *God grant me the serenity to accept the things I cannot change,*
> *courage to change the things I can,*
> *and the wisdom to know the difference.*

It just makes so much sense. I accept that I will never fully understand women. It takes courage to examine my deficiencies and change myself. And it takes wisdom to know when to approach a woman and when to back off.

I have recently learned to accept that my wife's idea of money management is different from mine. However, I can and do share my concerns and manage my money in the way I think is responsible. I also know that it is important to let my wife enjoy her shopping as this makes her feel good about herself (shopping is also a form of entertainment for her).

The biggest element that I was trying to change (unsuccessfully) about my wife was her take on reality. She was most impressed when I got that her reality was different than mine, and said I was going to let her have it (her reality that is). It also lifted a burden from my shoulders as I no longer felt responsible to correct her, in my view, misguided ways, and it made for a lot less arguments. In other words, it became a lot more serene in the house and in my heart. I was now more accepting of her and her interpretation of reality. It did not mean I agreed, but I accepted that she could have a vision different from mine. My ego learned it would not die if my wife and I saw things differently. What a relief!!!

So, if you want less arguments and a more peaceful household, practice the Serenity Prayer. Use it to calm yourself, use it to open your heart and use it to give yourself perspective. Perspective is a form of wisdom. To be able to stand back and see what is happening outside of the desperate screams of our ego takes discipline and courage. Taking perspective also allows you to distance yourself from the emotions of the moment and lets your heart and mind have a chance to participate in the action and not just react out of your fears. As I said, I love the Serenity Prayer.

Patience

Patience comes about when you do not have to be right and your actions are coming from the heart. Love is eternally patient. As in the Bible:

I may be able to speak the languages of human beings and even of angels, but if I have no love, my speech is no more than a noisy gong or a clanging bell. I may have the gift of inspired preaching; I may have all knowledge and understand all secrets; I may have the faith needed to move mountains – but if I have no love, I am nothing. I may give away everything I have, and even give up my body to be burned – but if I have no love, this does me no good.

1 Corinthians 13:1-13

When coming from love there is no need to be angry. We might get sad when we see loved ones hurting themselves but when coming from love we understand that they have a personal path of learning to follow and we accept this as painful as it may be. We might share our concerns, even strongly, and let them know what we think and how we feel, and share our love for them – but then we back off and let them do what they will.

To be able to do this is to understand how little control any of us have in the world. We control ourselves. Other people control themselves. If you try to control other people you will get a lot of drama in your life. If you want peace and quiet – stop trying to control other people and learn to control yourself.

When you do this you will have the space and time to observe others and hear their wants and needs. This leads to understanding. The less I try to control my wife the more I hear her needs and can take action that supports her, the more love she feels towards me, and you know where that goes. It goes into a better relationship, a more secure relationship, a more intimate relationship and a more sexual relationship.

There is another benefit that you get as well. Because your wife is spending far less time fighting you, she now has the time to see what your needs and wants are. You see, it goes both ways. Don't wait for her to go first. Be proactive and shock her drawers off!

Understanding

Patience leads to understanding. Because you have stopped trying to control her, stopped dominating the conversation (if you do), are less combative and more open to listening, you will hear, maybe for the first time, what she needs. You will start to understand her reality. Thus, you will be able to support her instead of just giving advice.

Support

Give to receive. I hear this every day in my business networking forums and it works on the home front just as well. An important element that should not be forgotten is that even when you give there is no guarantee that you will receive support *in a way that you identify as support*. It may come in other forms that you may not recognize or appreciate. Therefore, you must tell your partner specifically what you want. For example, "The kind of support I like is when you _____." This could be: listen to me, give me feedback, find the logical errors in my point of view, and encourage me to succeed. This way she knows what works for you. Do not assume that she can read your mind (even though women can be very good at this) or knows when you need support (men are very good at not expressing their needs).

There is another and deeper question to be examined. Do you know how to receive support? Many of us find it difficult to receive support because even admitting we need support is to admit weakness and/or failure. "I should be able to do this on my own." We have fallen for the North

American myth of the heroic individual. If you want to be a loner then learn never to accept help.

Business has discovered that "teamwork" is essential for success. The home is no different. If you want success in your relationship, have your partner be part of the team. Learn to trust her, rely on her and feel free enough to consult with her and be supported by her. Two heads are better than one and two pairs of hands can lift far more than one.

Partnership

Your team of two is a partnership. The Oxford Dictionary defines partnership with words like *associated with and sharing risks and profits and companion.* Your partner can be all of these things. In our marriage vows some of these issues are brought to light as a list of expectations and obligations which are stated out loud and the public acts as a witness. If you are not married, or have not done this even if married, I recommend making up a list of expectations and obligations. Both you and your partner can do this separately and then share your list and then draw up a mutually agreeable list. This list can act as your touchstone whenever you lose your way in the relationship. It can act as a reminder of what and why you got into the relationship in the first place and what were your commitments.

I have been in business on my own and with partners. Having a partner is a lot more fun even though more risky. It takes ongoing communication to keep a partnership healthy and happy. If you like to give orders – have employees. Just remember, your partner is not an employee and will not like to be ordered to do anything. Consulted yes, ordered no!

Freedom from Verbal Attack

As you can see from the section on partnership, if you are treating your loved one like a partner, odds are that she will treat you in the same way. If not, you have to encourage your partner to look at her behavior. If she is unwilling to change her behavior you have to decide whether or not to change the relationship.

Assuming that your partner appreciates the wonderful way in which you treat her in the relationship she will undoubtedly treat you in the same way. You may have interesting conversations, even passionate discussions, but you will not be personally attacked. There is no need to make a personal attack when the underlying ground between the partners is filled with mutual respect.

This is the key – respect. Do you respect your partner? If you don't, you will not have a satisfying relationship. But do you respect her? I don't want to skip over this question because it is easy to say, "Of course I do." Or to say, "Of course I don't." I have many male clients that have no respect for women and this influences their relationship. It is much easier to put down someone you don't respect than someone you do respect. It is much easier to get angry at someone you don't respect than someone you do respect. It is much easier to abuse someone you don't respect than someone you do respect.

More sex

Despite what you hear, not every male wants more sex. Many do, but according to my female clients who are shedding tears about their husbands lack of sexual desire – many men don't want more sex. Research shows that women's libido reaches its peak in the late thirties, just when men's starts to drop. I had a friend, a big time womanizer, who once said to me, "I do it once a week but once a month would be fine." We are all different in our needs.

On the other hand, most men I know would like to have more sex than they are getting. Where do you fall on the continuum? Are you getting enough? Do you want more or less? What are your real needs? Do you even know what you want or is this driven by our sex obsessed culture? This is a lot of questions. Let's tackle them in reverse order.

Q: *Do you even know what you want or is this driven by our sex obsessed culture?*

A: What is a healthy sex drive? I don't know. Does it mean I have ten children? Does it mean I am insatiable like a Greek satyr? That satyr would now be called a sex addict. Men in North America seem to be addicted to viewing, talking, thinking and wishing about sex all the time. No wonder we don't get enough sex. We are too busy engaging in secondary sex-related activities and not engaging in the primary act with another human being.

Here's a wild idea. Maybe we should just ask our partner for sex more often. Even better (so I've been told by women), don't ask, just set up the situation to be more conducive to sex. This includes romantic dinners out, candle light dinners at home, massages, etc. If you don't know what makes her more receptive to engaging in sex – ASK! And make a LIST. Heck, I'll help you out – with the list, not the sex.

Tip: *Men want sex to be intimate; women want intimacy to have sex.*

What Makes My Partner Want More SEX!

1) _____

2) _____

3) _____

4) _____

5) _____

I have known the above tip for many years but it was only recently that I understood it better. My wife explained to me that in order to accept a foreign object (my penis) into her body she needed to be relaxed. If she is worried, anxious or tense, this makes it difficult – both emotionally and physically. In order to drive home the point, she said. "Don't you think you would have to be relaxed if I was going to stick a 6 inch dildo up your butt?" Point well taken. I got it. Men penetrate, women are penetrated.

Summary:

You are important too, and creating a list of what you want is as important as what she wants. It is also helpful to know what you don't want and what your bottom line is. In order to help keep you on track and know the difference between making a difference or not, the serenity prayer was examined to see how it applies to having a relationship with a woman.

> *God grant me the serenity to accept the things I cannot change,*
> *courage to change the things I can,*
> *and the wisdom to know the difference*

Allowing a woman her own reality will go a long way to lessening arguments and creating more love in the family. It is also a lot less work for you. It takes effort to convince someone of the errors of their ways and embrace your all-knowing and wise belief systems. Having patience makes the process of improving your relationship a lot easier. As I said, if you want peace and quiet – stop trying to control other people and learn to control yourself. Patience leads to understanding and this allows you to become supportive. Because you are demonstrating patience, understanding her reality, and being more supportive, the partnership between you and your wife is strengthened. Furthermore, as your relationship is enhanced you will notice some dividends. One, there will be less arguments and two, there will be more sex.

Chapter 8

HOW DO YOU COMMUNICATE WITH WOMEN?

The single biggest problem in communication is the illusion that it has taken place.

George Bernard Shaw

The first question should be; how do you communicate with women? It is important to establish your current interactional style. You can't go from here to there if you don't know where here is. So where are you? What are your strengths and weaknesses when communicating with women? Which women are problematic for you? Your wife, co-workers, cashiers – all of them? Write it down.

<u>Women I Find Difficult To Communicate With</u>

1) _____

2) _____

3) _____

4) _____

5) _____

Now we examine the difficult part. What is your problem or difficulty when attempting to communicate with women? Maybe it is hard when . . .

- she gets emotional
- you get emotional
- when we talk about the kids
- when we try to talk about sex
- when she starts yelling
- when you can't think of anything to say.

Examples of your behavior when conversation becomes problematic might include: I clam up, I get angry and shout, I get violent, I leave the house, etc. You get the idea. Now, begin this list by starting with the word "I".

My Difficulties In Communication Happen When

1) _____

2) _____

3) _____

4) _____

5) _____

After you have identified what you think are the problem areas, go to your girlfriend/partner/wife and ask her what she thinks are the problem areas. Write them down.

What My Partner Thinks Are My Difficulties In Communication

1) _____

2) _____

3) _____

4) _____

5) _____

Do not at this point let her see your list (you may not have anything on it or she may disagree and you don't need to give her another reason to dump on you). Then thank her. Do not argue with her but if you have any questions ask for clarification. Watch out for pulling faces and eye rolling. Remember, the body talks.

You will now have a list of areas which are problematic for you. Because, if you had nothing on the list, she did, and if she has nothing to offer you are in really big trouble. She either does not think you are serious or she doesn't care anymore (I'm assuming it's not because you have a perfect relationship). Either way you are in trouble.

If she doesn't care anymore it's time for a lawyer and if she doesn't think you are serious 1) tell her again you are and ask her to fulfill your request and 2) if she doesn't, say "Thanks" and realize the proof is in the pudding. In other words, you will have to show her just how serious you are by your deeds. It's time for action Spiderman and action speaks louder than words. Most of you will have something on this list. If not, talk to others about where you can improve your communication skills.

Now compare the two lists. How much is similar and what is different? Which items do you agree with and which do you not agree on? Keep both lists. You will start working on the items that you feel are most detrimental to effective communication (e.g., calling her names and swearing at her. So will saying, "You're just like your mother.").

My Strengths

Here's another list. Oh stop groaning. If you don't write it down it is in one ear and out the other and you know it. This one might even be fun . . . or not. It is a list of your strengths. This list will help you get through the tough times. When your beloved is ragging on you for being totally incompetent and saying that you will never learn to communicate, that is when you look at this list. Some examples are: I work, I am on time for meetings, I play with the kids, I make a mean omelet, I know how to change a tire, etc. If you have more than ten examples put them in your log book or journal. But definitely write them down. If you can't think of any, ask people you trust and record what they say – don't argue.

<u>My Strengths</u>

1) _____

2) _____

3) _____

4) _____

5) _____

6) _____

7) _____

8) _____

9) _____

10) _____

If you are really brave, ask her to write out a list of where she could improve her communication skills. You will write one for her as well. Do not tell her you are doing this. If she asks, say you will, but you can't give it to her until you have worked on a few things first, and you will keep it for further discussion. Now, if you and your partner already have high level communication skills feel free to share right away. For the rest of us, hold back unless you want a fight.

Defensiveness and Ego: Knowing is not enough

Let's be honest here. Figuring out or having someone tell you where you need to improve yourself are things not easily heard. If this is true for you, that is your ego feeling the pain. The ego likes to be in charge, invulnerable, and has a tendency to be selfish as well (I am using ego not as the psychologist would but as it has come to have meaning in everyday language).

Why should we feel pain just because we are not perfect? Yet we do. Not being perfect *means* something. And if others know our weakness, we fear they might exploit our vulnerabilities for their own ends. Our ego is constantly on the look-out for how it can maintain a superior position and not get in an inferior one. The problem is that it is not connected to reality. As the cowboys used to say in the old days, "There is always someone faster than you."

The ego can, and often does, get in the way of a good relationship and better communication. If you believe that men are smarter than women and your wife is faster at adding up sums than you, instead of just accepting this reality you will question her figures, pretend you have the answer or put her down. In other words, you will make her feel inferior any way you can so that your belief – men are superior to women – stays intact.

Unfortunately, this keeps you stuck, outside of reality, and makes you a lousy communicator. Effective communication is based on truth (as best you know it), your feelings, and wanting to understand the other. It is not based on having to win. Become a lawyer if you have to win.

In order to protect itself the ego sets up defenses. These defenses protect the ego by setting up a wall. It is hard to communicate when there is a wall between you and the other person. This wall separates you from the other by creating a boundary. You are on the inside and she is on the outside. Communication is difficult when there is separation and armed camps – when you are in two different territories.

Here is a list of the common tactics the ego uses to defend itself (with apologies to Freud).

Denial

What problem? If I ignore or pretend it doesn't exist I won't have to deal with it. The problem with this tactic is that the problem just gets bigger with time. The problem only goes away when she walks out the door (I see it all the time) or so you think. What really happens is that you take the problem into the next relationship.

Intellectualization and Rationalization

If we are forced to concede that there is indeed a problem we can reduce the emotional impact by rationalizing it. Women hate this one as they listen to us use logic and focus on minutia, while missing the essence of what is happening.

Projection

What anger? You're the one with the anger problem (screamed at the top of his lungs – projection). Projection is when you place on others what you have difficulty accepting in yourself.

Regression

If you notice that you throw temper tantrums, or go and lock yourself in the room and pout, or say "Fine, I'll go play by myself" while grabbing the deck of cards, then you are regressing into an earlier childlike stage of development. You are acting immature because you don't know how to handle a situation or the feelings that come up (often hurt, anger or embarrassment).

There are a number of other defense mechanisms, but these are the obvious ones that can be readily identified by you or others, and because of their concrete attributes they can be changed more easily than the more complex defense mechanisms.

Getting clear

Just so we are absolutely clear, you should now know where your challenges lie and with whom. If you haven't written this down here is another opportunity. What do you do? Make a list of problematic behaviors.

<u>Problematic Behaviors</u>

1) _____

2) _____

3) _____

- When do I do it? This is a list of the conditions when the behavior erupts. For example, "When I drink. When she is nagging me. When I haven't eaten."

1) _____

2) _____

3) _____

- Where do I do it? Where do the disruptions usually take place? For example: the house, at work, in the car.

1) _____

2) _____

3) _____

- How often do I do it? This is simple. Whenever we talk, once a day, once a week or once a month. Interestingly, frequency is not always a good predictor. You may argue a lot but if it is constructive it is not necessarily problematic. On the other hand, you may argue once in your marriage – as the person is leaving for good. This actually happens and usually from people who say, "Oh, we never argue." How often do you argue? ___x/wk.

• Why do I do it? This is a tough question. There may be many reasons so put down the ones that typically crop up for you. Examples include: "I feel my integrity is being questioned, I am furious that she doesn't believe me, and I think she should do what I say." It is important to be honest even if your answers are politically incorrect. Identifying your beliefs is critical. Then, and only then, can you examine them to see if they are getting in the way of effective communication.

1) _____

2) _____

3) _____

Commitment for change

Are you committed to change? I know you have some desire as you are reading this book but change is a lot harder than reading or talking about it. Change is effortful and requires courage, and if not courage, then at least high levels of motivation. Saving your marriage or relationship is a powerful motivator. The process of becoming an effective communicator with the opposite sex, and especially with your intimate other, is a daily practice. There will be countless opportunities to practice what you are learning in this book. So don't get discouraged. Use every engagement as an opportunity to learn, to grow, and to get closer with the one you love.

Change theory

One way of thinking about change theory is as an *unfreezing* of current attitudes, beliefs, and behavior. Then a learning process occurs during this unfrozen state, and finally a *re-freezing* of the new way of being – from frozen to unfrozen to re-frozen (for more info on this process see Kurt Lewin's *Field Theory in Social Science*).

There is no doubt in my mind that the change process requires a letting go of old behavioral patterns that have gotten us into our present predicament. Once we open up to the possibility of change we can start to see where we have gone wrong and learn new ways of managing the situation. When this is done we need to practice what we have learned and, rather than the re-freezing as suggested by Lewis and Schein, we need to remain flexible enough to continue absorbing new data as the situation evolves. Our partners are not theories. Quite the opposite. They are ever shifting human beings and even though they have typical behavioral patterns, these are subject to change, especially as they adapt to our changes. If we stay in the refrozen state we could shatter like ice.

Maintaining a certain plasticity and flexibility will enhance our ability to communicate effectively and not fall back into old patterns. We do indeed need to "set" the new learning acquired and realize it is an ongoing process.

Review with partner

This is extremely important to do. Reviewing the plans with your partner increases the likelihood for success. Having said this, it is possible to achieve your goals without telling your spouse what you are up to. You may have your reasons for not sharing... especially if you feel that she will not believe you and give you more grief than if you just went ahead and showed her the results.

Other than a few narrowly defined reasons not to share, I encourage it. It will be like having a co-captain, someone to share ideas with and analyze how the game plan is going. She can be your greatest cheerleader as well. And we guys love cheerleaders. On the serious side, your partner and you will be able to assess, on a regular basis, what is working, what is not, new strategies to try, and you will be able to debrief each other.

Strategies for success:
- Confer with partner
- Pick one thing
- Timeline
- Do it
- Celebrate
- Assess and re-commit
- Make out (it's worth a try)

Assuming your partner is in on the game plan as stated above, you will use her skills to achieve the goals you have stated. She will feel part of the team and have a vested interest in your success. She will feel important that you have confided in her and trust that she will help (this does not mean that she can tell you what to do all the time – set up clear rules of engagement on how she is to help).

Pick one item on your list that you will work on. Let's say it's listening without interrupting. Work on it until you feel confident that you know how to do this, and then go on to the next item. Build on small successes. Make sure she is part of the process for identifying when you have accomplished a goal.

Log book

As you may have guessed by now I am a proponent of writing things down. Making lists and recording behaviors is the only accurate way of tracking your performance and identifying what works and what doesn't as well as being able to see patterns as they emerge. Guess work is not enough, especially if you have a partner who has become extremely critical of your efforts. It is satisfying to be able to show her in black and white that you only lost it once last week, whereas you normally lose it five times a week. This is an improvement, whereas she may have been steaming over that one incident and not realized that this week was indeed better than it has been in the past.

Daily review

To help use your log book make a habit of writing in it once a day at which time you will review the content and assess how it is going. Again, if it feels right include your partner, if not on a daily basis, at least once a week. Think of the daily review and log entry as a sailor shooting the sun with a sextant to identify his location. It is comforting to know where you are and where you are going.

Weekly review

Once a week look at what you have done. What worked and what didn't? Are there any patterns? Where do you need to go now? What needs to change, be reinforced, or dropped altogether? The weekly review is your way of tracking your progress or lack thereof, making adjustments, and giving yourself encouragement as you move closer to your goals. It is also a time to make new commitments (goals) to yourself and your partner as you rack up the accomplishments.

Summary:

In this chapter we identified how you communicate and what were your strengths and weaknesses regarding communication. Furthermore, we identified which women you have difficulty with and what are the particular circumstances in which these difficulties arise.

Once this has been accomplished you then took the lists to your partner (if it is safe to do this) and enlisted her in your program of communication improvement. With luck, she will have given you insight into her reality and you will have added new items to your lists. If your partner is really supportive, and a player, you can get her to do the lists as well and discuss them at a later date once you have mastered your communication skills.

Self-improvement can be difficult and the main stumbling block is our Ego. Denial, intellectualization, rationalization, projection, and regression are some of the ways the ego tries to defend itself from change (which the ego sees as death – definitely something to be avoided).

In order to make these changes, motivation is crucial and a dollop of courage useful to help you endure the difficult times. To make the process easier it is helpful to think of unfreezing your current attitudes and beliefs, taking on new ones and then, if they work, refreezing the new ways of being. However, you will need to remain flexible as change can happen quickly and often. If you are unsure of the effectiveness of your actions, bring your partner into the picture and ask.

Finally, strategies for success include: identifying what you will work on, work on it, have a timeline, keep a log, assessment, and celebrating your wins.

Chapter 9

STOP, LOOK AND LISTEN:
WHAT WOMEN WANT IN COMMUNICATION

Communication leads to community, that is,
to understanding, intimacy and mutual valuing.
Rollo May

Listened to

What do women want in conversation? They want to be heard – to be listened to. It is vitally important that you learn to – Stop, Look and *Listen*. How hard is this? Very hard from all the complaints I hear in my office. Men just seem to have a hard time shutting their mouths and listening. I know I do. I like to talk. I'm quick and have a solution for every problem that my wife comes up with. Unfortunately, this doesn't work for her. What's a guy to do? LISTEN. Yup, that's step one.

If it was this easy we wouldn't have the problems we do between men and women in communication. So what gives? Part of the problem when we have known our girlfriend, lover, wife, mother or sister for any length of time, is that they are predictable (as are we) in what and how they communicate. We are bored of the same old same old, whether it is a complaint against us or a comment on the latest fashions. We are bored and tune out.

Some men have mastered the art of appearing as if they are listening.

They even look at the other person, nod their heads and put in minimal encouragers like aha, yes, really, and no kidding. Are they really fooling their partners? I don't know, but probably not. She has just accepted the charade as it is more acceptable than him watching the TV or staring at some pretty young woman walking down the sidewalk.

And the guy? He is missing out on a real relationship with his wife. At least he could be honest and say, "Hey honey, what do you think about the situation in _____?" (put in your favorite disaster zone of the day). Oh, she is not interested in world events. No problem. Ask her about something that is relevant to both of you. It could be the kids, the new subdivision, the vacation, the new car/dishwasher you want to buy, a book you or she has read or want to read, whatever. Just pick something that interests both of you. If you really want to take a risk, ask her what she thinks of the relationship. That ought to stop her in her tracks – at least for a few seconds as she tries to decipher if you are being serious or not. Now that you are talking about something in which you have some interest it will be easier (or should be) to listen to her thoughts on the matter.

Key points to remember. *Don't try to change her mind. Ask questions like: could you tell me more, how did you come to that opinion, and what makes you feel that way. Ask questions that expand the topic and are open ended (not yes/no questions). Pick up on an element of what she says and expand on it and explore it further with her. Listen and listen some more. If you hear yourself talking for more than 30 seconds stop and redirect the conversation to her.*

Respect

Step 2 is like the famous song by Aretha Franklin – R-E-S-P-E-C-T. Respect goes a long way in keeping a relationship healthy and facilitating communication. It is like axle grease reducing friction. Gottman's [40] research indicates that respect is the key to having a successful relationship. If respect is missing the relationship will fail.

If you do not have respect for your partner, now would be a good time to examine why not. Has she not lived up to your expectations, has she become a monster in your eyes, does she exhibit behaviors that have made you lose respect for her? Or is it that you just don't respect women? If it is the latter it is probably obvious to her how you feel and not only does it get in the way of effective communication, it affects the relationship negatively.

Again, I will use the business model. If you don't respect your partner, you will either ignore her, manipulate her, or get rid of her. If she feels your disrespect and is a strong individual she will confront you to work it out. Likewise, you will have to confront yourself to identify why you feel the way you do and make some hard decisions as to why you are in a relationship with someone you don't respect.

No solutions please!!!

Women want to be listened to not given answers. I know, this goes contrary to everything men know about problem solving. That is the key – problem solving. When women talk to you about a problem they are rarely looking for an answer from you. Even if they did want an answer it would not be the one a man would offer. Our answers rarely take into account the complex issues of relationships the way women perceive them. We tend to see relationships simply. Women see relationships as complex webs of emotional exchanges that are at the core of meaning making. Men just want a solution. Don't offer it. Instead, listen, explore, identify her feelings, and get clarity. Through this process of astute questioning she will feel understood and have more clarity about the issue.

Ask what they need

When in doubt ask. For heaven's sake don't tell them what she needs or should do. Or the greatest mistake a guy can make – tell her what she is feeling. Ask!

Loved whatever the issue

When going into a "discussion" with my wife I try to open up the talk with a statement about how much I appreciate and love her. This does two things. One, it reminds me that I do love this person who, in the moment, I may feel like doing horrible things to, and two, it lets her know that whatever I may bring up, underneath it all, I love her and I am bringing up the issue in order to get to a place of harmony and greater understanding. Saying "I love you" can go a long way to facilitating open dialogue.

If she is instigating the conversation, knowing that you love her will create openness and a willingness on her behalf to share her concerns in a less defensive or aggressive manner. It becomes a sharing rather than a fight for survival.

Safe space (non-judgmental)

Having love as the ground of being, in a conscious and overt way, creates a safe space. It is a space in which you and she can openly discuss . . . anything. In psychology we call this "unconditional positive regard." No matter what is brought up, we honor that person's right to have their experience – whether we agree with it or not. This is of course easier said than done at times especially if her complaint is about you. It is hard not to get reactive.

A safe space could be taken literally. You and your partner could decide beforehand on an area in the house where you have these talks or arguments or discussions or fights. There are a number of advantages to this. As you go to that specifically identified space the body and mind prepares for the encounter. As you get ready for the meeting you can remind yourself of your love, the outcome you want, and the rules of engagement which can be read out loud before you start or posted on the door. This room is a special place and a sense of ritual can be a part of the process.

Every now and then my wife and I wrestle (and we are not young) just to get out our aggression towards each other. We end up laughing and having a great time. It connects us physically and it acknowledges our anger in a safe way. Whoever is the stronger must dial down their strength to match the other's and be willing to let the other win a move as often as they do. This is great practice in learning that winning is not really the point of it all, but rather getting back into a place of love.

Stop, look, and listen

Stop, look, and listen means exactly what it says. When a woman is trying to have a conversation with you, she wants you to stop whatever it is you are doing, look at her, and then listen to what she has to say. If you can make yourself do these three little acts you will be ahead of almost all the men on the planet. Let's look at these items point by point.

Stop. To stop watching TV, working on the computer, or reading the paper is not an easy feat. Research [41] tells us that when watching television our focus, or mind-shifted-mental state, is like being hypnotized and less able to make analytic judgments. It takes an act of will to break free of the spell.

For our female readers, please don't expect your partner to snap to wakeful attention the first time you call his name. It won't happen. If he says yes on your first call, that is simply a reflex. His mind is not there – not even close. It is important that you (the woman) focus on making sure you have his attention before diving into whatever it is you want to say.

Look. When your partner calls it will be to your advantage to pull your attention off whatever it is you are focusing on unless a) it will cause you to lose a finger b) it is the last 30 seconds of any sports game. If it is the last 30 seconds tell her what's happening – it's the last 30 seconds – and that you will be available immediately afterwards and if it is really important to put a note on your lap – on second thought, make that your hand, she might be a little rough.

Assuming it is not the last 30 seconds of an important game, help yourself and 1) use the mute button or better yet, shut off the TV, 2) look at her with a gaze of love and not absolute loathing at being torn from your heavenly bliss, and 3) say, "What is it dear?"

For our female readers, how do you know you have his attention? When he is looking at you with a constant gaze. Not flickering back and forth between you and the TV. Best results are obtained when the TV is put on mute (guys can pretend to listen while looking at you when they are in fact listening to the play by play) or even shut it off if the conversation is going to take more than thirty seconds (and as one of my female editors reminded me, there is always the PVR).

Finally, to make sure he has heard, ask him to repeat what you just said. Now remember ladies, you are trying to communicate with some-one who a moment ago was in a hypnotic-like trance. This is not the best opportunity to be heard. You may want to reconsider your timing and if you have no other options (you have to go to the store right away and you are letting hubby know that the dog has to be let out or there is going to be a mess in the kitchen) stick a written note somewhere. I recommend on his lap or in his hand – the two are often connected, he is bound to notice. Sorry for the digression guys. And finally . . .

Listen. You may have to repeat your acknowledgment (What is it dear?) as she could be stunned into silence. Keep your focus up and the process will last only a few seconds. Listen to what she says. Repeat it back as it usually involves instructions of some sort. And for best results, write it down on your handy pad that you keep on the side table at all times because you know this always happens and that you will promptly forget what she has said as soon as you re-focus on the TV.

Treat her as valued partner – think business

Women want to be treated as if they have a brain in their heads. They want respect. They want to be treated as equals and all that that means. They want their opinion to matter. They want to be listened to. They want fairness and equality. They want to be treated as a valued partner in the relationship.

If you are ever unsure of how to treat your wife or sense that some-thing is not right, just ask yourself if you would treat your male business partner the same way. If you answer, "No," then you need to re-examine your actions and make changes immediately. Starting with an apology would be a good idea.

Don't argue when it is not an argument

What does this mean? It means that many of your arguments don't even need to happen. It takes two to argue. Many times it is simply our need to:

- Be right
- Be in control
- Show who's the boss
- Avoid feeling in a one-down position.

And this gets us into an argument. Our egos don't like to be told what to do. We may be defensive because we are being asked to take out the garbage ... when we said we would do it yesterday. It may be just an old habit.

Whatever is the reason; if you want to have fewer arguments it is in your hands, or rather, in your breath. When your partner says something that riles you:

1) Take a breath. This is critical as it will give you time to think and calm your physiology down.
2) THINK. Ask yourself, is this worth arguing over or is it just my automatic response and my need to be right, in control, the boss, etc.?
3) Breathe again and listen if she is talking and then paraphrase or ask questions to understand her position.

Don't get angry at her for who she is

We all have faults. If she doesn't close the cupboards, or is not the cleanest housekeeper (hey at least she is doing it – not every woman does), or has some annoying habit, remember that she is human. She is struggling just as you are to be as happy as possible in a difficult and complex world. Being a woman has issues that you and I will never face and some we will never understand. Have *compassion* instead of trying to mold her to your idea of what she should be and how she should live her life.

When you come from this place of compassionate acceptance she will feel it – believe me. She will feel safe and will respond in kind. She will start to treat you differently and in ways that will make you smile. And all because you took that step of acceptance.

Does this mean that you have to agree with everything she says and does? Of course not! But your disagreements will occur in the context of unconditional positive regard. It is not her that you have the problem with, but the action or behavior. This distinction is critical as no one responds well to character assassination.

Ask questions

As I've said before, women do not want solutions given to them, or to be told what to do, or to have you get frustrated at them for not picking up on your brilliant suggestions. It just makes them feel bad, which is the opposite of your intentions. Remember, they are not like us in how they want support. Don't do it the "guy" way.

One of the best ways of avoiding the common pitfalls of men/women miscommunication is to ask questions. Be careful that you don't sound aggressive in the questioning or ask too many questions too quickly. To get best results start your communication with a feeling statement (if you have a good idea of what she is feeling, otherwise skip this). For example, "Gee honey, it sounds like you are really **upset** with what Mary said to you at work." Pause and listen.

If there is an uncomfortable silence, ask for clarification, "Is that how you feel about it?" This is to confirm your assessment. If she doesn't agree you get to listen again. If she agrees, and depending on how much information she has provided, you might venture another question like, "were others involved (a bridging question)?" When you have all the facts and the context of the situation, which will take some time, what you will notice is her emotional state will have shifted. Indeed, she may have come to some internal resolution (which may not be visible to you) and is ready to move off the topic.

At this point you take a breath and see what she comes up with. Women often discover their thoughts and feelings about the situation while talking about it. Surprisingly (to us guys), after exploring the situation they will decide not to take action. The solution is in their understanding of the relational dynamics of the event. Once they understand that, they may or may not take action. Men almost always want to take action and don't only when they feel there is not enough power on their side.

A mantra I try to remember at these times is, "Exploration not solutions." The difficulty for men is in coping with our anxiety. For us, solutions and knowing what action to take reduces our anxiety. Try not to take on her problem. Often, she doesn't even see it as a problem (so why is she crying?) in the same way that we define a problem.

Make time – later never happens

Communicate now. This instant! As the old saying goes, tomorrow never happens. Putting off a talk, a disagreement, an argument, a fight, whatever you want to call it, only heightens the probability of increased tensions and negative outcomes. The longer the delay the more you pay.

Some people put off arguing for years. Some people never argue and think this is a good thing. It is a disaster. Knowing how to argue is a basic survival skill and keeps a marriage healthy. Fighting, in and of itself, is not the major determinant of a successful or unsuccessful relationship. The biggest factor is **respect**. Some couples fight a lot, some don't. What is important to remember is not how much you fight but *how* you fight. Respect is the key when managing conflict with your partner.

Most women, not all, want to communicate now. Sound familiar? Whenever you can, follow their lead on this. First of all, everything is fresh. Coming back at it two days later . . . hell, I can't remember what we were arguing about after a ten minute delay, never mind two days. So it is to your advantage as well to discuss it ASAP. Second, why carry around a bunch of unprocessed feelings and unfinished business. That just leads to indigestion and moodiness.

Don't belittle, dismiss, joke, or put-down

Nobody likes to be put-down, dismissed or be the butt of a cruel joke. I don't like it, you don't like it, and your wife doesn't like it. So why are you doing it? We usually engage in this kind of behavior when we feel like we are losing an argument, to gain control of a situation or to let someone know we can abuse them without consequence – we have the power.

Jokes are often used to put people in their place. And if there is a negative reaction or push back we say, "Don't be so sensitive, I was only joking." We have all seen this and the joker may indeed not be aware of the impulse that is driving the joke. The jokes are often insults protected by a layer of humour. The teller may be unaware of the anger that is fuelling the need to tell the joke.

Belittling comes in many forms: a pat on the head, calling her baby, giving orders. Anything indicating she is less, and you are more, is belittling. Like joking, belittling can be camouflaged as affection. Patting her on the bum in public may be an affectionate gesture in your mind but it also sends the message to her and others that you can touch this woman when and where you please. In essence, this is my property.

Clarification point: *If she pats your butt and you pat hers and you both like it – no problem. I'm all for fun and displays of affection as long as the other person is comfortable with it. If you are not sure, ask. I learned this one the hard way.*

Try to understand

We all want to be understood. Trying to understand a woman is probably the biggest challenge you will ever face in your lifetime. Some say that it is an impossible task. Yet, your partner does want to be understood by you in the same way you want her to understand you.

We have covered many ways that can improve your odds of understanding her but in the end a full grasp of a woman's reality may not be possible. It is a little bit like perfection. Just because you cannot achieve a perfect state does not mean you can't strive for it. You may never be perfect but you will be better for having made the attempt.

In the same way, work hard for understanding. After all, you can relate to pain, sorrow, and anxiety – all aspects of suffering. Those emotions and feelings you share in common with your partner. How she experiences these challenges and tries to overcome them may be different, especially in how she relates to the interpersonal dynamic, but that does not mean that you cannot try to grasp her unique viewpoint. And even if you fail she will love you for the attempt.

Summary:

To recap, women want to be listened to and respected for what they think and say. They want to be heard for the essence of what they are communicating and not be trivialized because their experience was not as you think it should be.

Listen for understanding not for solutions. If in doubt, ask for what she wants and don't make assumptions. Coming from a place of love and unconditional positive regard will create a safe space for the both of you to share in meaningful ways. If needed, designating a specific room in the house as the sharing or communication room can be useful.

When starting a conversation remember to stop what you are doing, look her in the eyes and listen. This little phrase **Stop, Look, and Listen** will save you countless arguments and headaches by ensuring enhanced communication between you and your partner.

Remember you are trying to understand your partner not win the argument, be right, be in control, or show her you are the boss. This is your ego trying to maintain dominance and it may work in the short term but reduces the quality of the relationship and ultimately leads to failure. By not trying to control her you will find that you get less angry and come to appreciate her for who she is and not for what you want her to be. As she feels your acceptance she will respond in kind and be more affectionate.

Asking questions and not saying or telling her the solution is the key to supporting your wife when she needs your attention. When she has an issue with you, don't delay for a better time. There is no better time than now. These kinds of conversations don't feel better later – usually it gets harder and harder the longer you delay. Think exploration and understanding and not solution when in discussion. Never belittle, dismiss or put down your partner when she is being vulnerable (this is a trust killer).

Chapter 10

BASIC COMMUNICATION SKILLS

No one is as deaf as the man who will not listen.

Ancient Proverb

Definition of Communication:

Succeed in conveying information or evoking understanding. (Oxford)

Communication is the transferring of information and the evocation of understanding. Men seem to have the information part down pat but fall short on the understanding aspect. *What's to understand but the facts themselves?* Men are solution providers. Give us a problem and we want to fix it. That's the way we are. So why don't women want our solutions? *Because they are not asking for them!* Take a breath. I know it seems like they are asking. They come to us as we are watching the football game, ask us – oops, seem to ask us about some problem at work or the PTA meeting and we give a simple no-nonsense and quick solution that is easy to implement. And what do we get for this. A lot of flack is what we get. What are we to do?

First: Communicating involves not only language but the use of the voice including tone, loudness, pitch and body language. The oft thrown about statement that 93% of communication comes from non-verbals is a modern myth stemming from the research of Mehrabian and Ferris [42]. Their research has been taken so out of context that on his website Mehrabian attempts to rectify the misunderstanding and inappropriate extrapolations of his work (there is a clear and easy to read article by Ian Brodie on this issue at:

http://ezinearticles.com/?Debunking-the-Myths-of-Non-Verbal Communication&id=974778). The upshot is that there has been an overemphasis on the value of non-verbals. Content is vital and yes, non-verbals do contribute to the overall message received, but not as much as is widely reported.

When communicating feelings and emotion, non-verbals do influence how the communication is received. Therefore, you must know what you are doing with all aspects of your communication. This may be difficult if you have never thought about or listened (i.e. believed anyone) when they said you talk in a sarcastic tone. "What are you talking about?" said with lip curled up and a slight whine.

If you are really brave, have someone follow you around for a day with a video camera. This could be the biggest shock of your life when you see yourself. I recommend you do this whether or not you think you have a problem. It is a mind blowing experience to see how others see you.

A less drastic step would be to conduct a survey of your partner, friends (male and female), kids, parents, co-worker and any other people whose opinion you value. This survey can be given in person or emailed. To increase the reliability or truthfulness of the responses, have them mail it back and tell them not to sign it. You may recognize this process as it is commonly known in business as a 360 degree performance review. The difference being that your survey is focused on one item – communication.

The survey could be as simple as asking the reader what they see as your strengths and weaknesses in communication. A little preamble stating why you are doing the survey and how their feedback is important to you is important to include. You may notice some patterns. Maybe your co-workers think you have high abilities but your kids think you suck. It is possible to be a good communicator with some groups and not others. Or are you consistent across groups. Are there differences between male and female responders? This is extremely valuable information.

Effective Communication:

Communication is a process in which everyone involved receives, sends and interprets messages all at the same time. Effective communication involves not only talking, but active listening. This can be difficult as there is almost always **emotion** attached to information giving. The basic elements of communication include:

1) Talking
2) Deep Listening™
3) Body Language
4) Metatalk (statements about how the communication is going, e.g., "this is upsetting for both of us, isn't it?")

Let's examine these four aspects of communication:

Talking

Some guys are talkers and some aren't. Both can be problematic. Which one are you around your spouse?

Talkers:

If talking is easy – great. Half your problem is solved IF your talking is:

- On topic
- Respectful
- Non-controlling
- Free of absolutist statements (e.g., You have to do this! No one in their right mind would think like that)
- An exploration of both sides of the discussion
- A discussion not just an argument
- In control of your emotions (you can be emotional but you are not using your emotions to manipulate or threaten your partner)
- Inviting the other person to talk.

However, if talking is a method of dominating and just trying to get your way this is not so good. If you tend to talk for more than a minute at a time you may be, what I call a *monologist*. You do not let the other person engage with you. In other words, you avoid the dialogue. You give lectures, make pronouncements, pontificate, and tell people how it is.

Non-talkers:

Big problem! If you have always been this way you may need to examine when this started as most people were talkers when young and then, for some, this gets extinguished. It might have been a dominating mother, father, sibling or family culture – *children should be seen and not heard* – these are all possibilities.

Or maybe you have difficulty talking to a woman. Again, this will be rooted in past beliefs. Do you believe that women don't deserve your efforts, that they should listen and obey, or are you afraid of their anger?

In the rare instance, you may be one of those "shy" people. For you, interaction with others has been genetically programmed as something to be cautious about. In all circumstances, you can learn to communicate effectively. You learned to brush your teeth and tie your shoes. You learned the skills to succeed at work. These skills are not hard-wired. But you learned them. Likewise, I know you can learn to communicate.

Deep Listening™

What is Deep Listening™? It is an intense, focused giving of attention and listening while actively processing information to understand content, emotion, and direction (where the person wants to go with the conversation – what they need). Deep Listening™ includes the following elements:

1) Confirming that what you think you heard is what she said. This can be accomplished by paraphrasing (examples in a few pages).
2) Differentiating between "emotional" content and "message" content
   • Emotional content
     • "Are you feeling angry/hurt/sad about/at . . .?"

- Message content
  - Meaning of what she is saying
  - "Are you saying you want things to change?"

3) Encouraging
- Encouraging the speaker not discouraging her.
- Say things like: "Tell me more, could you explain that, I see, now I understand, that's interesting . . . "
- Use minimal encouragers: these are sounds of encouragement like, "Aha, ahhh, yes, go on." This indicates that you are following the conversation and with the person.

4) Focusing your attention on the speaker. This means:
- stopping what you are doing
- looking her in the eyes and
- listening.

Don't Discourage by:

- Interrupting while she is talking
- Saying things like, "That's stupid, where did you get that idea, unbelievable"
- Rolling your eyes, looking away, reading the paper, walking out
- Using reactions that threaten or close down the conversation:
  - Staring at her like you are about to attack
  - Expressing anger in a threatening manner
  - Throwing things
  - Screaming and swearing.

Body Language

Think about it. If you are sitting in your favorite chair, arms folded and back towards her – what do you think you are communicating? Certainly not, I'm interested in what you have to say. Similarly, rolling of eyes, finger tapping, grimaces and fidgeting all convey disrespect, irritation and wanting to get away. You may indeed want to get away but would you act this way if you were in a meeting with your business partner discussing some difficult (or minor) problem. I think not. He'd wonder what the hell your problem was. Your intimate partner also wonders why you are so unwilling to interact. This is usually because of past conditioning and or the inability to communicate effectively and have emotions at the same time.

Eye movements, facial expressions, signs, signals, and body posture constitute body language. Let's examine each of these in turn.

Eye Movement:
- Focus on the speaker – not the TV, the girl walking down the street, the ant crawling across the floor – look her in the eyes.
- Keep your eyes still. Eyes darting back and forth look like you are trying to escape, hiding something, impatient or distracted. Focus, focus, focus!
- You might break eye contact naturally if you are thinking about a point or a response but make sure to come back to her eyes as quickly as possible.
- Don't bore into her with undue intensity. This makes the listener uncomfortable and your job is to make her as comfortable as possible so that she can communicate freely and fully (this will also speed up the process so you can get back to whatever it was you were doing before). Look at her with active interest and

warmth in your eyes. If you can't muster the warmth, neutral will work.

Special Note: *Looking in the eyes when someone is talking is culturally specific behavior. In some cultures it is considered a sign of disrespect.*

Facial expressions:

- Smile. Smiling is more than good, it is great. There is nothing so inviting as a smile as long as it is genuine. On the other hand, there is nothing so disheartening as a scowl or the mask of death. What is the mask of death? That look on your face that is so devoid of emotion that it makes Freddy Krueger look like a nice guy. You think it conveys nothing but it is the exact opposite. Check it out in the mirror sometime – scary. Conversely, don't put on a fake smile. It will be interpreted as you not taking her seriously.
- Grinding your teeth and jaw-clenching. Either one is distracting in its own right and can be interpreted as being tense or angry.
- Don't pull faces, snap your head back, or shake your head back and forth (clearly meaning no, non-agreement, or disbelief).

Signs and Signals:

- Scratching, cleaning your eyes and ears and picking your nose or teeth are all signs of disinterest and disrespect. Don't do it.
- Watch out for clenched fists (threatening), doodling, and tapping or drumming of fingers (impatient or bored).
- The famous middle finger sign when you rest your head in the palm of your hand.

- Quickly crossing and uncrossing of legs. Either you have to go to the bathroom or you want to be anywhere but there.
- Falling asleep (it happens and the consequences are predictable).
- Walking away, stretching, and yawning.
- Loud or not so loud vocalizations or sounds of disinterest (e.g., *Oh boy, here we go again, yeah* – said with biting irony or sarcasm).

Body posture:
- Slouching, slumping and generally draping yourself on the furniture in too relaxed a manner indicates you not taking your partner seriously.
- Arms folded over the chest is conveying the opposite message of being willing to listen. Watch out for the justification that it is a comfortable posture. It may indeed be comfortable but sends the wrong message.
- Standing with arms akimbo (on your hips) is a challenging posture.
- If sitting, be in an open posture with feet uncrossed and slightly leaning forward (but not aggressively).
- If standing uncross and relax your arms – watch out for personal space. Do not stand too close to your partner and tower over her whether she is standing or sitting.
- Be aware of overall tension in the body. Try to relax and if that is too much try not to get super tense.

Metatalk

Statements about how the communication is going (e.g., "do we ever get plugged in when we talk about this subject"). This might sound like stating the obvious but sometimes the obvious needs to be acknowledged. It indicates that not only are you listening but hearing at a deep level (e.g., "talking about this is really upsetting you?") or at least being able to identify the dynamic between the two of you as in the first example. This is so far and above the average inter-gender communication that you will win major brownie points.

Overcoming non-listening habits

You might be thinking at this point that there is an awful lot to remember. I never said it would be easy, just worthwhile. The easiest way to remember the important hints on how to communicate with women is to remember what our mothers' taught us when crossing the street.

1) Stop
2) Look and
3) Listen

Stop whatever it is you are doing: watching the TV, reading the paper, working on the computer or your son showing you his X-box, or Sony Playstation. **Look** at your partner – in the eyes and with love if you can muster it and say, "What is it dear?" or "How can I help?" or "Yes" and then **listen**.

If your partner decides to talk to you in the final few seconds of your favorite sports event go to the hyper-speed version of Stop, Look and Listen. It goes like this. Quickly stop looking at the TV, look her in the eyes and say, "Honey, there's officially 20 seconds left to play and it's a close game. It will take about five minutes before it really ends. I will talk to you right after the game is over. I'll then be able to give you my *undivided attention*. Is that OK?" (at this moment keep looking her in the eyes until she answers – if you avert your eyes, you lose).

Now, assuming she agrees, you make sure that you go find her and have that talk right after the game ends – not after the post-game show. Also, be as accurate as possible in how long there is left in the game. Finally, if you know you will forget that she has even talked to you, at the end of your statement or after she agrees to talk later, ask her to make sure you don't forget. This could include, if you want to have fun, things like, "And if I forget throw yourself in my lap," or "tickle me," or "spray me with the water bottle," or some such thing where she gets your attention in a dramatic or humorous way.

How to Listen
1) Listen: Deep Listening™ – stop what you are doing, turn off TV, look in her eyes and listen for content, emotion, and direction.
2) Listen: Don't interrupt – hold off insightful questions, rebuttals, analysis, solutions, and good ideas. Avoid the lecture and don't preach or pontificate.
3) Listen: Identify feelings, don't tell her what she is feeling or how she should feel or think.
4) Listen: With respect, ask clarifying questions (but not "why" questions).
5) Listen: Clean out your ears of judgments, preconceived ideas and beliefs.
6) Listen: With your body – face her, uncross arms and legs, lean

forward as if interested, don't roll your eyes, and be conscious of facial expressions.

7) Listen: Without changing the topic or taking over the conversation.

Note: *Taking over the conversation can occur as a demonstration of dominance or as a demonstration of shared experience. Dominance or one-upmanship is obvious. The shared experience process is more subtle, or not, according to my wife. For example, your wife shares an experience and you immediately want to say, "Me too, I remember when . . . ." Even though well intentioned – I have a similar experience and can relate to you – the end result is still taking over the conversation and shifting the focus away from her and on to you. I used to do this all the time. And even when it was pointed out to me I would argue that I was establishing commonality. Not so, my partner would just get pissed at me for taking over the conversation and shifting the focus. The time to share a similar experience is after she has expressed herself fully. If unsure, ask. For example, "That's amazing; I went through the same thing. Is there anything else you need to say about what happened?" If she says no, then, if it was a significant event, ask if she would like to hear your story. When you share your story, keep her in mind and the focus of your telling. It's not about you at this moment in time.*

Minimal encouragers

While Deep Listening™ you can promote your partner's self-exploration and re-enforce the fact that you are actively engaged by uttering what is known as *minimal encouragers*. These include sounds, single words or short phrases like: ahh, unhuh, hmmn, yes, I see, go on, etc. This process is a way of participating with the other through encouraging and short communications that keeps the conversation moving without interrupting. You are an active participant. When you listen actively, a powerful message is sent. The message is:

- I am willing to listen
- You deserve my attention
- You are lovable
- You count
- You are OK
- You are important
- I care about you
- You have a right to your feelings
- I want us to succeed.

Furthermore, this kind of active listening demonstrates or shows good faith and encourages the other to listen to you. You might actually hear something new or important. Deep Listening™ focuses the discussion and reduces the potential for an escalation of conflict. Finally, it reduces defensiveness and resistance.

All of the above elements will make your partner feel incredible. The first time this happens she may go into shock. If this happens, just sit there with an innocent smile on your face and ask, "How are you feeling honey?" Double shock! At this point there is a good chance that she will either burst into tears or jump in your lap and start kissing you all over. And all you did was **listen**. Assuming you don't get carted off to bed right away, you may have to participate in the conversation.

What to do after you have listened?

Paraphrase. This is step # 2 in the process. Paraphrasing is stating what you think your partner said. There are two elements in what a person communicates: 1) the content or what happened and 2) the emotions or feelings.

For example, "So, if I heard you right, you and Bev had an argument at work about who should be responsible to talk to the new secretary about how to dress appropriately and you are upset with Bev for making you do it even though the secretary works for Bev. Do I have that right?" Your partner will now say "yes" or "no" and give you some modification of what you said. This goes back and forth until you have paraphrased with 100% accuracy. When this is achieved you LISTEN again as your partner continues the story.

The **only** time you get to interrupt is when you feel there is too much info. What you say is, "Excuse me honey (or your favorite endearment), I just want to make sure I'm understanding everything and I don't want to get lost. You said that . . . " and then you paraphrase up to that point. She says yes you got it, or corrects and you re-paraphrase until correct. This process continues until she is finished her story.

You don't have a lot to do other than listen and paraphrase and remember what is being said. What might happen, and it doesn't happen often, but if it does, I want you to be ready for it; she may ask you what you think. Be careful. Keep your answer succinct and don't be quick to offer a solution. The best way to answer is to:

1) Start with an overarching statement like, "Wow, that is a difficult situation."
2) Identify her feelings (anger, guilt, etc.) and be tentative about

this and seek confirmation at the same time. For example, "and it sounds like you felt trapped into having to deal with the problem and you resent Bev for putting you in this position."

3) Next, ask her if she has thought about how she would like to handle the situation (notice you haven't offered a solution).

This will be the hardest part because men usually have at least three good options at this point in the conversation. Your partner will probably have a response or she might need to talk it out more or even delay and need to sleep on it. DO NOT PRESS FOR A SOLUTION. You have already done a great job in supporting her the way she needs to be supported. She will love you for it. Typically she will say things like, "Oh honey, thanks for listening, I feel much better," (even if she has not come up with a solution – go figure), and then hug you. And be waaaay more receptive to making love.

The above example was the easy one because it involved someone else. What happens when the conflict is with you? The first stage is the same:

1) Listen to her complaint/upset/request
2) Paraphrase until you are able to clearly state what she is saying.

I have to interject here because a couple of reactions will most likely be occurring. First, you will probably have an **emotional reaction** to her complaint. You may feel attacked, angry, defensive, hurt, sad, helpless, no good, hopeless, cold, violent, etc, etc. You get the idea. You now have to deal with your emotional reaction to the event (your wife saying something). Really, it is no more than that, she said something. She uttered sounds that have meaning. And boy do we add stuff onto the literal meaning of the words said (she may indeed have added meaning as well by how she said what she said). However, you cannot be responsible for her stuff – only your own. Now, how do you deal with your reaction?

Dealing with your emotional reaction!!!

This is the deal breaker. I see it all the time. Even today as I write these words I have a client, who, no matter how hard he tries, cannot control himself when his buttons are pushed. He cannot manage his behavior (shooting off his mouth and trying to control what his wife thinks and does) when his emotions well up. Even though his marriage depends on it – he cannot do what is needed. His need for control and his inability to stay in an emotionally uncomfortable place (i.e., not knowing when she will come back, feeling insecure and anxious) makes him choose every wrong move. He cannot "understand" why she is not home with him. It is "unbelievable" that she walked out. Well, you had better believe it because until you do, until you are able to see life from the other person's perspective you are doomed. Doomed. Do I need to say it one more time – DOOMED!!!

Your emotions can hit you in the blink of an eye. They are fast. However, your thoughts are faster. It is in that quarter second gap between your emotion and action where you need to learn how to slip in a minimum of one thought, even if that thought is . . . breathe. Taking this one action will shift your perspective from being out of control to being in control. You *cannot* control your emotional reaction. You *can* control your response to it. You *can* control your behavior. You can control the expression of your emotions.

I used to work in a maximum security prison hospital. We had guys from across the country that were so difficult to manage in their home prisons they were sent to us for training. One of the areas I worked in was the Aggressive Behavioral Control (ABC) Unit. These men were extremely violent with little or no impulse control. They reacted instantly to any perceived threat. If someone looked at them the wrong way they attacked either verbally or physically. My challenge was to get them to think before they acted. In other words, to respond rather than react.

One of the arguments they used to justify their behavior was that they were not in control of their reactions. "It happens automatically. I'm not in control." They would often say. One day while in group session this excuse came up and I said, "Really, well tell me, if you were on the street having an argument with your wife and wanted to hit her but saw a cop standing across the street watching you, would you hit her?" He said, "No, of course not. Do you think I'm stupid or something? I would take her home and then beat the crap out of her." "Oh," I said, "then you are in control of what you do?" Slowly the lights came on as he realized that he was indeed in control of his actions.

Realizing that you can control your behavior is crucial. If you keep saying things like, "She made me do it, I don't know what happened, and I can't help myself," you are not taking responsibility. I know it's hard. When locked in an argument with "her" and the feelings come up, it feels impossible not to react. The control you so desperately want is not over her but over yourself. This can be learned. If murderers can learn it so can you. We all have had murderous thoughts and fantasies. The difference between us and those men in prison is that we have not acted out on them. If you can control these most extreme action tendencies, you can control other less dangerous behaviors. You can control yelling, cursing, pushing, hitting, and throwing things.

The first step is to realize that you have given yourself permission to act as you do. You are in control. If you are still not sure or don't believe this ask yourself if you would scream at your wife in the middle of a restaurant with your boss sitting at the table. Not likely. Then you are in control of your actions. This is a good thing.

Now, you have to tell yourself that no matter what, you will not do certain behaviors. Make a list of these behaviors and a list of what you will do when you feel/think you will react in the old way. This second list (interventions) might include things like: walking away, time out, taking a breath, counting to ten, and telling your partner that you are extremely upset and need a minute to compose yourself.

Behaviors I want to stop

1) _____

2) _____

3) _____

Interventions

1) _____

2) _____

3) _____

If you still find that anger is getting in the way of a healthy relationship do something about it. Read a book, practice the interventions and if necessary, take an anger management course or workshop. If this is not enough, look at individual and/or couples therapy. This may sound like a lot of work but it is worth it. Imagine a life where you have discussions instead of arguments and where love is the predominate feeling in the household. Priceless!

Emotions

Many people believe that if you feel a certain emotion, action must follow (e.g., anger leads to yelling, hitting, throwing things, etc.). In fact, if you learn that it is permissible to feel the whole range of emotions and you learn how to express emotions constructively, the chances of an emotion getting you into trouble decrease dramatically.

Originally, emotions were given to us for survival purposes. If danger threatened, the flight/fight emotions spurred us to action. Sexual desire ensured the continuation of the species. Affection probably welded a family unit together for mutual protection and benefits. As our brains, and then our societies, became more complex, we functioned more and more from learned behavior as opposed to instinctual. Our emotions became more and more complex and were governed increasingly by our thoughts and beliefs which were instilled in us by family and the society at large.

Further in the process of trying to live together, we learned a lot of rules about how we were supposed to feel. What are the appropriate emotions and how to express them for specific situations is a learned process. There is a lot of research on emotions and a variety of opinions on what are the basic emotions that we are born with. Two to eleven basic emotions with the average of between five and six [43] encompasses the body of research. Personally, I think the basic emotions are anger, sadness, happiness, fear, and anxiety with all other emotions a blend of these elemental feelings with some emotions socially/culturally created, like shame. Shame has to be learned as it is not intrinsic to human nature.

For example, how are you supposed to feel when told you are to head a new project at work? Happy and grateful is expected and you may feel this or something completely different depending on your personal circumstances. You might actually feel angry because you are overloaded and were given the job because Harry, who should have been given it, is incompetent so it has fallen on your shoulders. And because the CEO personally gave you the job and told you how important it was for the company, you smiled, demonstrated enthusiasm, and thanked him for his show of confidence and assured him you would complete the project successfully. We have become clever at showing one emotion and feeling another. We have also become clever at hiding from ourselves. We can ignore, neglect, discount, and rationalize our feelings. This process for men begins at an early age. Most boys, somewhere between two and three years of age remember the famous words that fathers utter when you somehow hurt yourself and were about to have a natural reaction and start crying. As I've said before, we were told not to cry and be a big boy.

That is where it all started – the denial of pain, fear and helplessness. If Dad was lacking in sensitivity, and many Dads were and are, he might have added, "and don't be a sissy," in a voice that was filled with contempt and disdain. The message was clear – do not show certain emotions – especially emotions that we later acquainted with weakness or being like women. Emotions that demonstrate a softer side were dangerous – you could be taken advantage of by others. The ultimate joke, and it is a bad one, is on us.

You and I have learned to hold in natural emotional responses. This takes effort. So much effort in fact that it can make us physically and psychologically ill. Witness the worker who puts up with disrespectful and hurtful behavior for years and then one day he breaks and goes, "postal." Witness the ulcers, IBS, alcoholism, drug use, and bad digestions that millions of American males suffer from in the daily pursuit of *the dream.* Not expressing emotions is dangerous to your health.

Summary:

Communication is the conveying of information or evoking understanding and, information without understanding is rather useless for most of us especially when trying to communicate with a woman. Communication involves not only the words but vocal qualities like tone and loudness as well as body language.

Effective communication has four aspects: talking, Deep Listening™, body language and metatalk. Once again, the essence to overcoming poor listening habits is the old Stop, Look, and Listen mantra.

Deep Listening™ involves:

1) Taking your attention away from what you were doing and focusing on her
2) Listening without interrupting
3) Identifying feelings
4) Being respectful when questioning
5) Dropping preconceived ideas about her or the issue
6) Supporting the process with appropriate body language
7) Keeping the focus on her.

The practical aspects of interpersonal communication are enhanced through the use of minimal encouragers, paraphrasing, and knowing how to deal with emotion – both yours and hers. If you have trouble controlling your emotions or other behaviors make a list of the behaviors you want to stop and a list of the interventions you will use to help you stop before you step over the line.

Remember, it is not the emotion that is problematic but how you handle it and the behavior that follows the emotion. The expression of emotion or lack thereof was taught to us by our families and our culture. Does your emotional expression work for you or against you? Does it help make you an effective communicator or not? Does it hurt you or help you?

Chapter 11

ADVANCED COMMUNICATION SKILLS

Most women aren't satisfied in a relationship
until they find a man who's truly communicative.

Hollandsworth [44]

You have now been introduced to the basic concepts of communication between men and women. But as you know, women are complex and all sorts of landmines await you when entering into the communication game. Let's examine some of the more advanced issues that can trip up even the experienced communicator.

What does she "really" want?

Have you sat there listening to your wife and wondered . . . what does she want from me? This is a legitimate question. If you are sensing that what she is talking about on the surface is different from what you think she really wants, it's time to voice your thoughts. However, **how** you voice your thoughts is critical and this is where many guys get tripped up.

Part of the reason is that your spouse may not know what the heck it is she wants. Or, she could be too afraid to directly state what she wants, or she may be so acculturated into an obtuse style of communication that asking directly may not be part of her repertoire. So, a gentle and subtle approach is needed.

If you are confused, this is great because you can voice your confusion without blaming (don't make your confusion her problem – focus on getting clear). For example, "Gee honey, I'm confused. Could you explain that to me more/in a different way, again, etc . . . ?" The point here is a genuine request for clarity, not to make her wrong because she is unclear, scattered, illogical or whatever it is you think has contributed to your confusion, even if all the above is true. Telling her she is illogical will only create animosity and decrease the chance of a successful resolution to the issue.

If, on the other hand, you do understand what she is saying but there seems to be more going on, you have a couple of options at this point. One, is to be upfront, but again say what you have to with a soft and loving voice, "Sweetheart, it seems that you want (paraphrase what you think she said and if she agrees say . . .) but I am sensing that something else is going on or that there is more to this. What do you think?"

Now, carefully watch her response. Watch her eyes and body language (is she shy? – maybe you have been talking about sex). Is she suppressing anger (be careful), or is she afraid (of you or herself)? If she is able to explore the issue – great. If not, you get to test out a few hypotheses by stating what you *sense, feel* or think might be the issue. After stating your hypothesis let her think and answer. You get to listen.

Another scenario is that she flatly denies that anything else is going on. There are many possibilities: she is telling the truth, is not telling the truth, is unaware of the truth, or you are misreading the situation (which occurs most often when men have a jealousy issue). This is what you do at this point:

- Give her another chance to clarify by asking, "Are you sure there is nothing else?"

Often, this will lead to an opening in the conversation. If not, you say,

- "Well, if anything comes to you, let me know. I am willing to listen." Then you stop probing.

This is, of course, difficult to do for most of us guys but anything less smacks of disrespect. Just to be clear, understanding another's reality doesn't mean you like it or agree with it. It is how *they* see the situation. It is their point of view – not yours. If you are going to get angry about it, effective communication becomes extremely difficult. If you cannot let go of the need to know a certain answer or cannot accept the answer given, this may be indicative of a serious problem and you may need to talk to someone about it. If you notice that you keep trying to prove to those people who are listening how your position is the right one, then you definitely have a problem and should see a professional.

In a sense, you are like a tourist at this point. The both of you are exploring the lay of the land but from a supportive stance. A stance that tells your partner that you are trying to understand her reality – not force your reality on her. She will be grateful for this approach and you will, with luck, have a clearer picture into her world.

Murphy's Law on communication states, *"If a word can be interpreted more than one way, it probably will be."* True in my experience.

With the Deep Listening™ process you should be prepared to understand and engage a woman with a fair degree of confidence once you have mastered the system. Now let's get down to the nitty-gritty of advanced communication skills. They are:

- Environment
- Jumping to conclusions
- Culture of the listener
- Past experiences of the listener
- Age
- Mood/emotional state
- Values
- Self-esteem (hers and yours)
- Sexist language and stereotyping
- Being a lawyer (making a huge issue on a minor or insignificant difference of opinion, mistake or error and absolutely having to win)
- Motivation
- Attitude
- Sticking to the point
- The past – don't bring it up
- Brainpower – using it to summarize

Let's examine each of these items:

Environment

Believe it or not, where you decide to talk to your partner can affect the outcome. Sometimes there is little choice in the matter and we have to deal with it then and there. However, if you do have time to think about where you are going to talk, here are some items to keep in mind:

- A space free from distraction (e.g., kids, TV, computer, loud noises)
- A space that is neutral (i.e., not your office) where both parties feel at ease
- At least two chairs and don't hide behind a desk. It is preferable to have nothing between the two of you but open space
- Speaking of space, it should not be a cramped area – that can increase tension. A place with a view creates a sense of openness and possibilities. Just be careful of using it as a distraction.

Jumping to Conclusions

This is a difficult one. You are a smart person and it is easy to see where a person is going in a conversation.

Warning: *It is just as easy to be mistaken. Even if you are right, BITE YOUR TONGUE. The other person needs to say what she is thinking and feeling and not be interrupted by your excitement, quick thinking or wonderful solutions. If you do interrupt – what happens? She gets pissed off or frustrated or gives up. This is not what you want to have happen.*

After she has finished speaking, you can 1) paraphrase and then 2) summarize what you think she has said, and if correct, inquire whether or not she is interested in your brilliant ideas. Personally, I wouldn't even go there – way too many landmines. Instead, I would ask more questions. For example:

- Where do you see this going?
- What do you want out of this?

- What do you need right now?
- Do you feel clear about it?
- Is there anything I can do to help?

Only after you have explored these questions, you might ask,

- Have you thought of any solutions?

Questions tell her you are listening and if you have thrown in an empathy statement first she will feel that you understand as well (this is winning you bonus points and we know where that ultimately leads – a happier relationship for both of you). For example, "It sounds like you are really frustrated with the situation . . .

- Could you tell me more about it?
- Can you clarify it more for me?
- What would you like to do about it?
- Are you feeling anything else?
- Where would you like to go from here?
- How does this affect . . . (fill in the blank)?

These are just a few suggestions. Notice that there are no WHY questions. Why questions are often meaningless and get people stuck in their head trying to find answers that are often impossible to answer leading to intense frustration and self-doubt. Go for who, what, where, and when questions. Also, try to have open-ended questions when appropriate. If the person is emotional, sensitive, or struggling to communicate use conditional words to ease conversation – words like could and would (never use should). To ease entry into a conversation even more you could say,

"Honey, could you . . ." Words of endearment can be useful to remind her that, a) you are coming from a caring place and b) you are on her side.

Culture

There are two cultures to be aware of when communicating with your beloved. One is the culture of her family when you share the same background and the second is when you come from two different cultures (e.g., British, French, Indian, Moroccan, Russian, Angolan, etc.). Sometimes, the differences are bigger between two families of the same cultural background than of different backgrounds. This tends to occur when there is a large economic gap between the two families and this may be reflected in different accents (even though speaking the same language), schooling, expectations, choice of friends, and general differences in attitudes, beliefs and expectations.

Even when you and your partner share similar socioeconomic histories there can be vast differences between families even in the same community. Maybe your family was into self-expression and the children were even expected to have an opinion and share it. Maybe your partner comes from a family where the kids were expected to be seen but not heard. Maybe your partner grew up with an alcoholic raging father or mother. Maybe talking about needs was just too dangerous and she has learned not to say what she thinks and needs. Or maybe the reverse is true.

When these kinds of differences exist we come to a situation or disagreement from polar opposite ways of being and with different beliefs as to how the situation will or should (there's that nasty word again) unfold. In these types of scenarios it is critical that you go slowly. Work through each item as it emerges. If she believes the guy should take out the garbage and you don't, see this as an interesting exploration for both of you. Where does this belief come from? What does it mean (e.g., guys are strong, they do the dirty work, and they do the disciplining)? How important is it for her that you take out the garbage? When do you have to take out the garbage? Now it's your turn to explore the meaning of, "taking out the garbage."

When a difference is engaged in from an orientation of discovery and exploration you can even have, dare I say it – *fun*. Yes, differences can be fun. If you doubt this, remember that the biggest difference is that you are a man and she is a woman and that is a whole lot of fun. Even if you can't agree, having some fun along the way will make negotiating more pleasant. In the above example you might trade off something (e.g., cooking) for garbage. If she wants some nights off from cooking it is only fair that you get some nights off from garbage or equivalent chore. This way you are making choices consciously, with both partners agreeing. This eliminates lots of problems.

The same ideas and concepts work with someone coming from another cultural background. Ideally you have discussed some of the issues prior to getting together as they can be significant. If she wants to eat East Indian food all the time and you like English cooking you have a problem. There are solutions of course, but the more these issues can be discussed before emotions become intense and before you are living together, the better.

Past experiences of the listener

The cultural and family backgrounds are essentially past experiences of the listener and have been covered. Other areas include dynamics between listener and mother, father, siblings, friends, community, place of worship and work.

We are the sum total of our experiences and we think that the way we see the world is the correct vision – reality. Surprise, it is only *your* reality. How you see the world may be similar to others or vastly different. It does not mean that the other person's view is wrong – just different. This is often a major stumbling block in relationships. I remember when my wife said to me, "Let me have my reality," one night when I was trying to convince her how her perception needed changing. That set me back on my heels. "Let me have my reality." Wow! I can imagine how disrespected I would feel if someone was trying to convince me that the way I saw reality was wrong. Yet, in my practice I hear this all the time – men and women trying to convince the other that their partners' perceptions of an event are wrong. I have even heard a client tell their spouse that she was not feeling what she said she was feeling. How outrageous is that. Yet it happens all the time.

Each person has had a unique constellation of experiences. When they see the world differently than you do, take the opportunity to explore how they reached the conclusions they have and marvel at it. It is a miraculous process and it is no less miraculous than the process that led to your own attitudes, beliefs and world view. Remember, this is your partner – use her unique vision to add to yours – not take away from it.

Age

How old is the person you are talking to? Obviously, you will talk differently to a child than to an adult. However, too often we continue to talk to our growing children as if they were infants when they have moved far beyond that in their cognitive development. Age, as a factor in adult intimate relationships, becomes a concern when the two parties are separated in time. I am a baby-boomer and you are generation X or Y.

Conflicts can arise out of a lack of understanding the spirit or mood of that age. Conflict can also arise from the older person having more experience (this doesn't mean they are wiser) and having done something many times whereas the younger person may be approaching an experience for the first time. The older person must be careful not to contaminate the experience whether by letting the cat out of the bag or putting their own past experience onto the event whether it was good or bad. It can be delightful watching the younger person learn and grow and move past events that you have previously encountered. The danger, as with parenting, is to not tell them how to do it by taking on the role of parent in these situations.

An upside of a relationship that has an age difference is that it keeps you younger. You learn all the current slang and get to see how this generation thinks and feels about the world and old farts like you. It is very humbling, I can assure you, having been there myself. The advantage for the younger person is gaining access to experience and stability.

If you are the older person the danger in communication is to assume you know more and dismiss the younger person for their lack of experience. Don't! Listen intently and with an open mind. You may be surprised. Your thinking may be as stiff as your joints. Open yourself to at least considering what is being offered and see if it makes sense from that person's age-group and it may even make sense to you if you are able to drop your habitual way of thinking.

If you are the younger person in the relationship try to have compassion for your older partner. On the other hand, don't be bullied into something just because they try to use their authority or experience to get their way. It has to make sense to you if you are required to do something. However, if it is something they want to do but just seems silly to you, maybe you can be generous and allow them their peccadilloes – after all, isn't that what attracted you to them in the first place?

Mood/emotional state

Let sleeping tigers lie. Likewise, don't try to have an important discussion when your wife is:

- on her period (if this is difficult for her – it isn't for all women)
- having a hot flash (women are often irritable when sweating for no reason)
- first thing in the morning (this applies to women who love their sleep. This may not be a problem for early-birds)
- if she is hungry (she may be hypoglycemic)
- _____, (your favourite example).

Let's assume none of the above applies and you are approaching her when she is well-fed and not totally upset about something. The challenging element (for most men) in having a conversation with a woman is that it can get emotional quickly. Then what do you do?

1) Breathe
2) Acknowledge the emotion – hers and yours
3) Determine if you are capable of staying in the conversation with such heightened emotion
4) De-escalate your emotions by:
   a. breathing
   b. taking a time out or
   c. talking with and through it.

Let's back up a bit here. When you go to have a conversation or even if she comes to you and you are not sure of her emotional state – **ASK**! "How are you feeling?" If it is obvious you can say, "Gee, you look upset about something." Even if she is totally upset at you, you are building bonus points by acknowledging her presence and validating her emotional state (do not comment on her emotional state, "What are you angry at now?"). You are to be non-judgmental, present and attentive. Women like this. You have entered the battle zone and indicated that you are not in a heightened state of war preparations. In fact, you are in your diplomatic uniform and assuming the best outcome even if we have to go through uncomfortable emotions.

Now, what about your emotional state? When you are upset you must:

1) Identify the feeling to yourself (angry, sad, hurt, whatever).
2) Breathe until you feel that you are managing the emotion.
3) If you are not managing the emotion do not start a conversation. Go for a walk, workout, whatever, but do not engage. However, if you do get into a conversation and it gets ugly and you have to leave, do not go without telling her why you are leaving and when you will be back.
4) Tell your partner how you are feeling at the top of the conversation, for example, "Honey, I was so angry I had to go for a walk (if you did not tell her before). I feel in control now and I would like to talk about . . . "

Sometimes we are in a mood: a bad mood, a down mood, or a happy mood. Obviously, when we are in a happy mood talking to our spouse is easy. When we are in an irritable mood it is questionable whether we should even begin a conversation. Sometimes an encounter cannot be avoided. Again, always state how you are feeling before you enter into the discussion. "Honey, I hear what you are saying and just so you know, I am in a foul mood so if I don't seem sympathetic or appear distracted – I probably am. Please don't take it personally. Sorry if I am not all here. I will do my best." If you are really in a bad temper, say so and re-book the conversation.

Values

Values are rarely talked about and are often hidden or assumed. What are your values? What are hers? Let's start with yours. Just so that we are clear let's define values first.

My Oxford Dictionary states that it is:

"One's principles or standards, one's judgment of what is valuable or important in life."

What is valuable, specifically about relationships for you?

Typical words and concepts include: loyal, honest, loving, caring, humorous, playful, spiritual/religious, intelligent, understanding, loves kids, etc. Put items that have meaning for you, not the small stuff. These should be, especially the top five, qualities that you cannot or are not willing to live without. You may only have three or four critical items. That's OK. Put a star besides the items that you cannot live without.

Put your top 5 on this list now.

<u>Values in Relationship</u>

1. _____

2. _____

3. _____

4. _____

5. _____

Now you have made explicit what has been implicit. You can look at your partner and ask yourself if she has these qualities. The lesser qualities are probably negotiable. If she doesn't put the cap on the toothpaste you will not die (unless you have OCD – obsessive compulsive disorder. Then, it may be critical that she has similar traits as you have unless you really want to expand your ability to accept her unconditionally on a daily basis).

If she does not have the essential qualities you have listed you are in trouble. Either you have to have a conversation about these items and see if she is willing to acquire them (e.g., loyalty – she is sleeping around and this doesn't work for you) and if not, you have to make some serious decisions. You can live in misery or get the hell out of there.

Self-esteem

When we have a low opinion of ourselves our ability to withstand conflict and confrontation is diminished. It is important to know where you are regarding self-esteem – low, high or in the middle. Also, are you high in some areas (work maybe) and low in others (arguing with your wife, dealing with the kids, or managing the in-laws). The value of knowing your self-esteem level is that you can prepare yourself when going into an encounter when you know that in that specific situation it is low. For example, you can prepare more, give yourself a pep talk and even do a mock run through of the situation with a friend. All of these suggestions will help you prepare for the event and knowing that you have prepared, in and of itself, will increase your sense of self-esteem through improved confidence.

If your partner has low self-esteem it is important to identify how it is expressed. Does she over-compensate and become belligerent or does she hide behind her passivity and agree (on the surface) to your every demand?

If she is passive and agreeable you can support her to speak her truth. Use a gentle and encouraging tone and listen to her when she speaks. Ask her to elaborate if she gives one word answers and encourage her by telling her how important it is for you to know what she is thinking and how she is feeling.

If she covers her low self-esteem with anger the work is more challenging in that you will have to manage your rising emotions while de-escalating hers. This is difficult for most of us. First, get your anger in control otherwise it will be the same old story – fight time. Once you have your anger in control you stand a better chance of resolving the issue. Focus on removing the threat. She is feeling threatened (maybe you argue better than she does, she may be afraid of being taken advantage of, old issues are coming up from her childhood and this is how she responds). Whatever the reason, work on showing her that you are not a threat by modifying your body language (get into a relaxed position, uncross your arms, sit, listen), let her rant on without interruption. When she appears like she might run out of steam ask her, "Is there anything more you want to say?" Listen if there is and if not, now you can engage.

Sexist language and stereotyping

"The weaker sex." Yeah, right! If they are so weak how come they live four to seven years longer than men on average? If they are so weak how come they outperformed men when NASA was training its astronauts and the men in charge buried the results from the public? Yes, men are larger and stronger on average. This difference has become less important in our modern age where physical strength is not a defining characteristic of success.

What is sexist language anyway? It is language that supports the belief in the inferiority of women. Notice I am not talking about the *differences* between men and women. There are plenty of those as described in earlier chapters.

When we are afraid of or don't understand someone we tend to find ways of dehumanizing them. It makes us feel superior. We do this in times of war (far easier to kill the other if they are subhuman/alien/foreign in some way) and when confronted by a minority that threatens us (think of all the racist language you have heard for Italians, Greeks, Poles, Chinese, Japanese, Koreans, essentially any race or culture other than your own). Now, I don't want you to get super guilty about this. All cultures/races do this. It seems, according to evolutionary psychology, to be part of our genetic endowment. It goes back to survival issues when we were in a tribal environment. However, we do have a brain and it has become incumbent upon us to be concerned with the survival of humans as a species and use that brain to override our primitive instincts.

And God knows, women are different . . . and scary . . . and powerful.

They are the creators of life. Men like to blow things up. We're good at that. We are also good at creating too. Look around at the world today – most of it has come from the minds of men. A Lamborghini is a beautiful thing. The highways of America are impressive even if ugly. The Great Wall of China and the Pyramids may be ancient but are astounding nevertheless. And building rockets and sending men to the moon – mind-blowing! Yes, we can create as well. But I digress. Back to women and sexist language.

The problem with sexist language, and we all either use it or think it, some of us more than others, but we do – is that it keeps us separated from women. It distances us from them by accentuating our differences. I mean, if monkeys are 98% the same as us genetically, women are virtually the same (the difference being that Y chromosome).

The solution is to become aware when you think or say something that puts women down or "in their place." Become aware when others do it and how you respond. Is it with an equally offensive remark or do you challenge it? The second step is to challenge yourself when you have a disparaging thought or say something offensive. Where does that belief come from? Does it come from your Dad, your friends, or society? Do you really believe that thought? If not, then why do you act as if you believe it?

Being a lawyer (i.e., making a huge issue out of a minor difference or insignificant error and absolutely having to win)

Acting like a lawyer is the biggest mistake guys consistently make when trying to communicate with women. The concept of lawyers was created by men and, until recently, was dominated by men. It makes sense then that it reflects our thinking – a male perspective on the world, what is right and wrong and concepts of justice and punishment. But most im-

211

portantly, it is a system of how to argue your point of view – how to win an argument. In a male world view this means logical, rational, using precedence and presenting your case with utmost conviction (whether you believe it or not) and a set-up or context that is adversarial in nature, not co-operative. It is a system where winning is everything and where if you have a weak argument you use technical loopholes to throw off your adversaries: delay, confuse, distract and resort to bombast if you have to, but whatever you do – DO NOT ADMIT YOU ARE WRONG!

Having worked with the judicial system I have often heard the phrase that we have a legal system not a justice system. This may be true. However, it better not be true in your household or you will have all the troubles that plague our current system. You know, things like riots, breakouts, and screaming matches.

Let us identify some of the bigger mistakes that acting like a lawyer entails and what we can do to correct this ineffective behavior when communicating with women.

1. Arrogance. Have you ever noticed how arrogant many lawyers act? Does it piss you off? Guess what, it pisses your wife off too. Stop it, NOW!

2. Detachment. Detachment can be seen as a calm demeanor or, in the extreme, a robotic ability to recall facts and figures in a monotone with a look of disdain or utter boredom on your face. I feel like punching this kind of person. Women find this type of detachment incredibly irritating. What usually happens is that they get more emotional and the guy becomes more detached and less emotional. This spirals to the point where she is either screaming or crying and the guy is thinking that she is a hysterical woman and why the hell am I trying to communicate with this insanity. The fix? Using your heart and feelings, stay connected to what's really important – maintaining a healthy relationship. It is not winning the argument.

3. Righteousness. It is a secure feeling knowing one is right. It is also an incredibly closed-minded place. One, it is possible that you may be wrong. Two, open up to the possibility that it may not even be about right and wrong. Maybe it is about understanding a different perspective. Maybe there are two rights. Maybe the right answer is something neither one of you has yet thought about and can only be revealed by engaging and exploring a completely opposite point of view. Be in the place of openness and willing to explore possibilities that you haven't yet contemplated.

4. Competitiveness. In the courtroom I want my lawyer to be competitive. However, in the home this perpetuates a constant state of negative arousal for both parties (unless you're one of those types who loves arguing just for the sake of arguing) and communication break-down. This does not mean that you will become pussy whipped – man's greatest fear. Most men do not want to be dominated by a woman and or be seen by his friends as having no back-bone. Unfortunately, this fear keeps us from being effective. We are so afraid of losing, being in a one-down position and being dominated, that we over-react and cannot accept even a well-intentioned and reasonable solution if it is different from our own preconceived idea of how it should be.

The solution is to realize that this is your partner you love and not the enemy. A solution needs to be created by both of you after all the thoughts and feeling of both parties have been explored and understood. Typically, at this point, the solution becomes obvious and who originated the idea unimportant. In other words, don't come to the table with the answer. Come to the table looking for a solution.

5. Having to win at all costs. This way of being leads to ridiculous things like, making up facts to prove your point. I've seen it and I've done it. Sad but true. Winning, or more accurately, the fear of having to admit you are wrong, will make a highly ethical person lie. That's right – lie. Lie with total conviction. Many women have heard these lies told with such force and for so long that they doubt their own sanity. This is not good for her or for you.

When you have to win at all costs, it costs you everything. You lose what is priceless – a loving relationship. The solution is to realize that you won't die if you have to admit you are wrong. The truth will not kill you but set you free. Is it painful? Yes, at first, and it will be until the ego comes to understand that there is a bigger game in town; a game in which the ego is a part of the whole and not the only thing. And that is the relationship.

Motivation: Are you motivated to have effective communication skills which will result in a better relationship with less arguments and more sex? "Of course I am" you say. Really??? Because there are costs involved and they are:

- Time
- Willingness to change
- Pain
- Confusion.

If you are willing to endure this trial by fire you will become a better man having been cleansed of your impurities. A new man indeed! One who feels secure, confident, and knows that he can communicate and because of this, have a special relationship with his partner. All growth involves pain as you burst the seams of your old skin and feel the tenderness of your exposed surfaces. Keep breathing as you practice these new ways of being. Have patience as you trip over your old habits. Forgive yourself and your partner when buttons are pushed intentionally or not. Keep your eye on the goal – better communication and a better relationship. If you do this, you will improve day by day, month by month, until one day you realize that you are arguing less and when you do fight it is over faster and solutions are found and resentments are dissolved. And, lo and behold, your wife is happier and you are getting more sex.

Attitude: "Attitude determines your altitude" is a popular saying that comes to mind when I think about this concept. A major component of attitude is our cognitions (thoughts/beliefs) we have about ourselves, life, others and whatever challenge we are currently facing (which could be your partner standing before you with a look in her eyes that would scare a rhino). Do you believe that it is possible to work it out with your partner or not? Do you believe that you can learn to communicate better, or not? "Whatever you believe," as Henry Ford said, "you are right."

If you believe in success you will do whatever it takes to become successful. There is one big assumption I am making here. That your partner wants the same success you do. If you both have the right attitude and skills, which includes a large dollop of respect for the other person, then success is assured.

When communicating with your partner, coming from love is the most powerful attitude to have. Or, as Friedman [45] said,

> *Communication does not depend on syntax, or eloquence, or rhetoric, or articulation but on the emotional context in which the message is being heard. People can only hear you when they are moving toward you, and they are not likely to when your words are pursuing them. Even the choicest words lose their power when they are used to overpower. Attitudes are the real figures of speech.*

Your underlying attitudes cannot be hidden. They emerge in every word and action you take. So, if you are not getting the results you want look deep inside and examine your basic belief structures and the attitudes that emanate from them.

Stick to the point: When arguing with your partner it helps if you are able to focus on the immediate issue and not bring up the way your sister treats her husband. You are deflecting the discussion off of you and complicating the issue by not so subtly telling your wife that she is doing it wrong and insulting her by comparing her to your sister. Wrong move Chuck! You will suffer until the end of time with that kind of mistake. Never compare your wife to anyone especially not to your mother, her mother or any other woman you know.

The need to waver from the point at hand comes when we realize that maybe she has a point. Men hate to lose an argument so badly that we will do whatever it takes to win and if moving the discussion off the topic is going to work – we do it. You will have to combat this almost instinctive response. Why? So that you work on what is of real importance even if it means acknowledging that your partner has a point. You will not be one down but one up for communication, the relationship and more intimacy (which leads to sex if you haven't figured it out yet).

The past – don't bring it up: Much like the point above, bringing up the past can be used to deflect the argument as a distraction or to hurt your partner or to add weight to a weak argument (if it were strong enough you would not need to do this). Bringing up the past is an unfair way of fighting. If you do this, it tells your partner that you do not really forgive. When we have a disagreement and work it out, or do something wrong in the relationship and are forgiven, to then bring it up again is to take back that forgiveness. How can you trust a person who does that? You can't. Furthermore, you engender resentment in the other person. This is adding fuel to the fire. Simply put, don't bring up the past in the heat of an argument.

Brainpower: If you are quick-witted, intelligent or able to argue persuasively be very careful that you don't trick yourself into thinking that you are right. Just because you are skillful, rational and logical does not give you the upper hand. Indeed, it almost puts you at a disadvantage. If you are this type of person it is easy to forget that your fellow human being is, like you, strongly influenced by their emotions. Women are culturally sanctioned to be emotional and we are taught to control our emotions. If you use what works with men in communicating with women, it will **not** work. Period!

Here is what you can do with your brainpower. Use it to penetrate what is behind the surface words being said. Listen to hear the emotional content of the communication. Paraphrase to clarify your understanding. Focus on her communication and not on your reactive response. Use your intellect/self awareness to identify when you are having a reaction and identify it. Use your brainpower to elicit what she wants from you and then direct your energies to providing her request. Summarizing what your partner has said is also a good use of your brainpower. Finally, use your brainpower to remind yourself that working through the issue leads to a much happier relationship. This is helpful when the communication is breaking down and you feel like pulling your hair out.

Summary:

Effective communication is a complex process and the more subtle issues explored in this chapter ranged from the environment, to culture, and to brainpower. Thinking about where you are going to have a deep conversation with your partner can enhance the likelihood of success. You do not need to be competing with the TV or the kids.

Learning to put our brain in slow gear or a state of Zen mind or beginner's mind helps to avoid jumping to conclusions. Use questions, paraphrase and summarize to enhance communication. Taking into account culture, age, and past experiences of your partner enhance your understanding of what may be influencing her experience and the way she communicates.

Knowing when and when not to have a conversation is critical to success and a difficult choice to make. Asking helps and picking up on obvious signals like hunger, pain, or moodiness will keep you out of trouble.

Knowing your values and being able to communicate them is critical to having a successful relationship. Being able to communicate your values leads to enhanced self-esteem. Likewise, you can support her self-esteem by not using sexist language or stereotyping.

Arguments are for lawyers and discussions for couples. Acting like a lawyer and needing to win is the worst thing you can do to become an effective communicator and improve your relationship.

Becoming an effective communicator takes a willingness to change, time, and involves pain and confusion. You will need the right attitude to manage yourself through the challenges involved. When discussing an issue stick to the point, don't bring up the past, and use your brain by staying focused, not on winning, but on improving the relationship.

Chapter 12

COMMUNICATION BLOCKS AND SOLUTIONS

Speak when you are angry —
and you will make the best speech you'll ever regret.

Lawrence J. Peter

Your emotions

Emotions are tricky. They are great to have as long as they don't get in the way of communication. They are even good for your health. Crying actually excretes toxins and tears have a different chemical make-up whether you are crying or laughing. Most men enjoy feeling happy, excited, and powerful. We don't like feeling sad, depressed or anxious. Who does? Some of us enjoy anger. It can be a powerful feeling or a feeling of helplessness or a motivator. What is it for you?

The difficult part of communicating when experiencing strong emotion is to stay logical and rational. In order to do this we cut off our emotions, however, this is problematic. Ever hear your partner say things like, "You're so disconnected" or "Don't you have any feelings?" You see, nobody wants to be sharing intimate thoughts and feelings with someone who is disconnected from their feelings. It is not safe.

What to do? The first thing is to not suppress the emotion. This is not easy if you cut off your emotion before it is even fully formed. I remember the first time I became aware of this phenomenon at a visceral level. I was having an argument with my partner. I could feel the anger rise up from my lower gut and just as it hit the top of my stomach, at about the sternum, it went sideways and disappeared. I was astounded. I was very angry and it just zipped away somewhere. This happened to be the place where I once had an ulcer from a traumatizing relationship, and where I still get pain when upset or anxious.

What emotion are you feeling? Identification can also be problematic. Is it anger, sadness, many emotions . . . what is it? In this case the first thing you need to do is *breathe* and *focus* on your experience – both body sensations and thoughts. The next thing is to state out loud what you discover. "Gee, honey, my stomach is all in a knot. I feel like puking and my throat is tight. I'm having the thought – run. Just get the hell out of here. I'm also thinking that we always argue over the same thing and it makes me feel hopeless." Not bad. Notice you are not trying to have an argument. You are not defending yourself or going blank or stonewalling. You are communicating your experience in the moment. This is how you overcome blocks to effective communication.

Now, you may be at the opposite end of the spectrum. You are someone who has no control on their emotional expression. It spews forth like hot lava from a volcano. If you are a take no prisoners kind of emotional guy, you have as great a problem as the unemotional guy – just in the opposite direction. Your first task is the same as the "what am I feeling?" kind of guy or the "I know what I'm feeling, I just can't express it" guy.

BREATHE! Breathe some more! And yet again. If this does not bring your temperature down to a place where you can have a reasonable conversation do what you do with the kids (assuming you control your temper with the kids).

Call a time out and leave the room for five, ten or twenty minutes. Make sure to:

1) communicate what you are doing (e.g., "I'm taking a time out for five minutes.")
2) return to continue the discussion
3) book in an anger management course.

Note: *It is still possible to have a hot or passionate or even a heated discussion and be effective. As long as you maintain respect for your partner. Respect has been identified as a key factor in determining the success of a relationship. If you show, or think in a disrespectful way about your partner, the relationship will most likely fail. The real question here is why would you be in a relationship with someone you disrespect? Or do you disrespect all women? And if so, where did that come from?*

If for some reason (e.g., kids, belief in the sanctity of marriage, time in, etc.) you want to continue the relationship, you will have to change your *attitudes* and *beliefs* about your partner and learn to restrain those negative aspects of the communications (e.g., putdowns, belittling looks or comments, noises of disgust, swearing, calling her stupid, ignorant, ugly or worse). This is hard to do if you really believe what you are saying. That is why it is easier to go to the source of your anger. *Look in the mirror.* Who are you really angry at? Are you angry at yourself for marrying her because you listened to your little brain and not the one on top of your head? Whatever it is, get a grip on the real causes and take an honest inventory of where you are in life and with your relationship. Keep doing the same old things and you will keep getting the same old results (until she leaves you and if she can't, life will be miserable – more of the same).

The second is to state what you are feeling without accusing or blaming the other person. This is done with "I" statements. "I feel really upset right now." Not, "*you* always make me feel so angry" (blaming).

Her emotions

I don't know about you, but when women cry I get a queasy feeling in my stomach. I get all soft and mushy, drop whatever I am doing, and try to take care of her. This can be a good thing or a bad thing. Depends on whether or not she is trying to manipulate me. That is the fear of course. Some men get suspicious when women default to tears. For me, it just plugs in the protector syndrome.

Crying is nature's response to the feelings of sadness or hurt (emotional and physical). Because of the negative beliefs about women and anger, it is not unusual for women to cry when angry (we have all heard the phrase – tears of frustration). Many women have expressed to me their difficulty in expressing anger generally and specifically with men. They may be afraid to provoke a violent reaction or are afraid of their own anger – just how much and how deep it goes. This can be confusing to men because we rarely cry (compared to women) and when angry we certainly don't cry.

What happens when she gets angry? Does this trigger a response in kind, do you back down, are you surprised, or do you take it seriously? In my culture angry women are not looked upon favourably (I don't know if angry men are either but there seems to be more of a stigma attached to angry women).

What's a guy to do when a woman gets emotional? Stop, Look and Listen. Stop whatever it is you are saying or doing. Look at her without any negative facial expressions (eye rolling especially) and Listen to her. She may be speaking through tears and, depending on your level of intuition, you can hold her while she cries. When in doubt, ask. Sometimes women don't like to be held when crying, especially if they are angry at you. Let her cry and stay present. When you feel it is right, ask her to put words to the tears. In other words, what is she crying about (said with concern not scorn)?

Essentially, what you are doing is acknowledging her emotions and not making them wrong. You are staying present which shows that you are not afraid of emotions or at least willing to push past your discomfort of them. You are not making her wrong which shows you have strength and compassion (you are not taking advantage of her vulnerability). This leads to trust. Trust leads to an increased understanding and depth in the relationship resulting in more openness, honesty, freedom and an overall sense of safety. And guess what, women who feel safe and loved are more receptive to – making love.

Your reactions to her emotions

This is a common block to effective communication. Your reaction to her emotion is where the breakdown begins. You see, she just had an emotional experience. That was hers. Your reaction to her emotions now puts the ball in your court.

Why is it that we can't just let our partner have her emotion? Because, it has triggered something inside us! What you do with your reaction determines who is in control – you or your reaction. I have no illusions as to how difficult it is to control an emotional reaction especially if we feel that our "buttons" are being deliberately pressed. An emotional button is jargon for the spot your partner presses to get a predictable reaction. It could be talk about your mother, what you promised but never did, your children's behavior, your erectile dysfunction (low blow), you get the idea.

Your button is "pressable" because it is an aspect of yourself that you feel uncomfortable with or inferior about. It is perceived as an attack by the ego. In other words, you don't react when your wife tells you something you know to be patently false. For example, she says you are physically weak and you happen to be a 240 pound weightlifter. You would probably laugh at this and wonder why she said it.

But when she says something that either has an element of truth to it or touches something within us that we are not comfortable about – look out. The demon rises from the depths of our being, rears its head and spews forth molten lava seeking to destroy all in its path. That response is for the aggressive types. If you are more introverted in your reactions you will clamp down on what you want to say, tense your jaw, give the evil eye and stomp out of the room to sulk silently (or not so silently) in the garage or some area deemed off limits to the woman of the house.

What's a guy to do when the button is pushed? First, take a breath. Second, identify what emotion you are experiencing. Third, share with her what you are feeling. Fourth, explore what is being triggered (e.g., insecurity). Five, relate and refocus this information back to your wife's original concern. In other words, once you have recovered from your reaction get back on task with your wife's original concern.

Family

When I talk about blocks to effective communication and mention family, I don't mean that they are literally getting in the way (though even that can sometimes happen). What I am talking about is all the learning that occurred when you were a child. What did you see, hear, believe and model as a child? It is this information that can get in the way of effective communication often without your realizing it.

How did you learn to treat women? Were they to be ordered around or not, did they do the cooking or not, did they do the laundry or not, did they do the disciplining or not, were they the emotional ones or not, who did you go to when feeling bad – mom or dad?

The same is true for what you learned about how men should be treated by women. Did Dad have the final say or not? Did Dad bring home the bacon or not? Did Dad have control of the paycheck or was it mom? How did Dad treat Mom – with respect or not? Were decisions made together or separately? Did Dad go drinking with the boys and was this upsetting for Mom or not?

As you can see, there are a lot of areas of potential influence and most of these teachings are in your subconscious. You are not even aware of them. You simply act on them. What's a guy to do? Well, by now you probably have a good idea of how I work so, let's make a list.

What thoughts and beliefs do you have from your family that get in the way of Effective Communication? Be aware of how subtle this process can be. Sometimes we say things like, "I hate the way Dad treats Mom. I'll never treat a woman like that." Really, and have you kept to that promise or, to your horror, find that you are treating your wife like that? Or, have you gone to the other extreme? You are so careful not to treat her that way that you have over-corrected and treat your partner with too much respect/deference/kid-glove type of behaviors and now you resent her because you don't communicate what you really believe at times. This can be just as problematic. Watch out for this one.

Now back to the List. List five items you learned from your family that get in the way of effective communication.

Here's an example: I learned that when my mother was emotional Dad got quiet, did not say anything, and often would leave the room. He was unable to engage her when she was upset or angry.

Note: *I learned this one to perfection. It took me until I was thirty-five to unlearn this habit. Prior to this, it caused my girlfriends no end of frustration because I was unable to communicate my feelings. I was angry and felt helpless in the situation.*

---

5 Items That Get In The Way Of Effective Communication

1) _____

2) _____

3) _____

4) _____

5) _____

Culture

We have explored this issue previously so I will keep focused in this section. When I say culture, I am talking about the beliefs that your particular racial/ethnic/national group hold to be generally true or appropriate. Each ethnic group will have generally held belief systems regarding how men and women relate and communicate. These traditional beliefs have held sway for thousands of years and only recently have they begun to shift.

What are the beliefs of your culture regarding the relationship between men and women? In this first question I want you to list the beliefs of the culture you grew up in. This may be different from what was held in your family. The reason I want you to identify these beliefs is because you were influenced by them, as you were influenced by what you saw and heard from your friends, radio, TV, movies, religious instruction, and magazines.

Here's an example: In my culture women cooked the meals and served the food. Your turn. List the beliefs of your culture regarding the relationship between men and women. Then, go back over the list and put a circle around the T (true) or the F (false) on each line to indicate whether your family acted in accordance to their cultural beliefs and then whether you believe or act as if you believe this is the way it should be or not. You will now have a schematic of the cultural belief, what the family believes and what you believe (with any difference between what you believe and how you act). If there is not enough room in the book, write it in your journal or log book.

The Beliefs Of My Culture Regarding Women

Culture   Family/You

1) _____ T/F   T/F

2) _____ T/F   T/F

3) _____ T/F   T/F

4) _____ T/F   T/F

5) _____ T/F   T/F

To understand your partner better, repeat this exercise with her even if you are from the same culture. There may be family differences and she may have different beliefs than you do. The only difference in this chart is the extra column where you indicate whether you think the belief is true or false.

Her Beliefs Of My Culture Regarding Women

Culture	Family	Her	You
1) _____	T/F	T/F	T/F
2) _____	T/F	T/F	T/F
3) _____	T/F	T/F	T/F
4) _____	T/F	T/F	T/F
5) _____	T/F	T/F	T/F

Attitudes

This is a tricky one. Attitudes are not the belief but how you hold the belief. Are you humble, arrogant, cocky, sly, demanding, pushy, confident or whatever? Do you have a positive attitude or a negative one? Are you hopeful or pessimistic? Put simply, if you have a negative attitude your chances of success in anything are lessened. Likewise, in learning to overcome blocks to effective communication, a positive attitude will enhance your chances for success. But what exactly is a positive attitude?

A positive attitude is the belief that one can improve the experience of a situation and/or increase levels of achievement. This is accomplished through mastering thoughts and emotions so that they are positive and self-enhancing. A positive mental attitude is achieved by focusing the mind on:

- The need for change
- Believing change can happen (this may require faith especially when there is no evidence for your belief)
- Identifying yourself as the originator of change and not the victim of life's circumstances
- Being aware of internal emotional states and changing or accepting them if they are inhibiting goal achievement but not being run by them in a detrimental fashion
- The willingness to let go of toxic beliefs and experiences of the self (i.e., self-criticism and using negative past experiences against oneself)
- Gratitude (at the very least for being alive)
- Being in the now
- Living proactively
- If you are spiritual, focus on the divine in the world and within yourself
- And finally, eliminating negative patterns of thought, speech and action and practicing positive thinking, speaking, and behaving.

This reminds me of that old quote, *"As you think, so you are. As you imagine, so you become, as you practice, so you better yourself."*

The need to know

This is similar to needing to be right. In this case, it is "knowing" the answer or the right approach or the best solution. Again, this refers back to our upbringing as kids and young adults where "being in the know" was and is a powerful place to be. So it becomes second nature for men to act as if they "know." They may indeed know. We know a lot or a little about a lot of things. And we are not shy about sharing what we think we know. Quite the opposite. We would feel like we were doing you (women) a disservice if we didn't tell you what we knew.

The problem is when 1) we don't know or 2) when we think the answer we know is the best for our partner or, horror of horrors, the woman knows better. In the first case, we are men and because of our training the last thing we are going to admit when trying to help our loved one is that we don't know. I *must* know. I have to know. My self-concept is predicated on being a man who is capable and knows. I know the score, I know how to make decisions, and I know what is best for those whose safety I am responsible for. It is a big responsibility but that is why we have broad shoulders (I hope the irony is apparent here). Being able to admit I don't know is as difficult as apologizing to a woman.

The need to problem solve

This need is so strong I sometimes wonder if it is genetic. It is certainly a male thing from a cultural and even a practical point of view (a male's perspective anyway). Unfortunately, or fortunately depending on your world view, how women conceptualize a problem and how men conceptualize a problem are two different things. We don't even have to go into the differences here. Trust me and look to your experience – it's different.

Knowing that men and women conceptualize a problem in a different way, we can stop trying to solve their problems from our point of view. It hasn't worked before so why would it work this time? The biggest challenge is biting your tongue. That hurts! Remember, doing the same old thing and expecting a different result is the definition of insanity.

Unless asked directly for your opinion or solution (and even then) your job is not to problem solve – it is to support. I know, I know, you think offering a solution is support. I think so too and it is true when dealing with men. But you are interacting with a woman and their concept of support is:

1) Listening
2) Showing you have heard
3) Identifying her feelings
4) Valuing her point of view
5) Helping her to explore the issue without being critical
6) Trusting her judgment (even if you don't)

Habit

Often we engage our partners in habitual behavioral patterns that do not promote effective communication, and we do this without thinking. It is simply a patterned and habitual way of acting. This is especially true if you have been in a relationship for any length of time. We develop shorthand ways of communicating. Unfortunately, we also develop shorthand ways of *ineffective* communication. We know what she is thinking, feeling or going to do. We are only half listening or worse, and when she starts complaining about how you don't pick up your socks, or don't discipline the kids, or don't – you get the idea – we go on autopilot and say and do what we always say or do. And you wonder why you find the whole process irritating. Act this way for many years and you won't even know how to have a real conversation with your wife – it will be a lost skill.

Yes, there is a solution. GET REAL! Have a talk with your partner on how you perceive and relate to each other. Tell her you want to change this. Ask her if she wants the same thing and is willing to engage in the process?

If yes, establish signals that both of you can use to alert the other person that they are acting in the old pattern (this could be a time-out hand sign, showing the hand, or a verbal cue). Make this part fun. Practice a couple of times to embed the cue. Give each other a hug and start. Practice and consistency over time is the key to changing an old habit.

Celebrate when you succeed and analyze the situation when you don't. Support each other. Repeat as often as necessary. That's it. Simple, but hard to do for most of us especially when the emotions flow. This leads to . . .

Being uncomfortable

A long time ago, my counseling advisor told me becoming a good therapist required the ability to withstand ambiguity. Likewise, to be an effective communicator, you must be able to withstand discomfort. It is uncomfortable when your partner is upset, especially if she is upset at you. It is uncomfortable when your partner hurls emotion at you. And it is very uncomfortable when emotions course through your body and outrageous thoughts flash through your mind threatening to erupt into a vocal onslaught upon your loved one.

Most of us hate these feelings and will avoid them at any cost. Unfortunately, that cost can be the relationship itself without our realizing it. Non-communication with our spouse is one of the leading causes of marital dissatisfaction which often leads to marital breakdown.

You have a decision to make. Are you going to keep avoiding these uncomfortable feelings or are you going to take a deep breath when they come up and stay present to yourself and your partner? You don't have to do it perfectly. You just have to be willing to engage the process and muddle your way through with these uncomfortable feelings. No more walking away, no more pouting, no more stonewalling, no more violent verbal outbursts, no more violence against inanimate objects, and no more threats of leaving the relationship.

Not understanding her

Do you honestly think I understand everything my wife thinks is important? Not a chance, and I have a good relationship. What I do that others don't is realize that what she is speaking about is *important* to her. This is so important I am going to repeat it. What she is speaking about is ... *important* to her.

Does she care or understand about my power tools. No. And I'm OK with that. This is not however an equal exchange. When she wants your ear over something you can't go, "Honey, you know I don't give a rat's ass about your new dress or how it fits." No. Some things in life are just unfair. In this case, you had better take an interest (or a least appear to) and come up with the right answer. Yes, there is a right answer in these types of situations. The right answer shows that you understand her needs.

Her needs? Yes, and they are usually quite simple. For example:

- She wants to be appreciated
- She wants to know that you think she is attractive
- She wants to be desired

- She wants you to think she has good taste
- She wants to know she made the right choice and on and on.

Like you, she likes strokes. We all do. Take a little time and make her feel good about herself. This will be pleasurable for you and her. Spread a little love around and you will see it come back in spades.

Time

We are all short on time. The lack of time is a great excuse for not dealing with your interpersonal problems. Working out a problem with another human being is time consuming. Working it out with a woman is painful and time consuming. The problem may not be time so much as pain avoidance. But, for the sake of argument, let's assume that you really, really want to deal with a problem with your loved one but you are really, really busy. Hey, let's make it even better. She is really, really busy as well. Great! Now we have two very busy people and they notice that not only do they have a problem (never having time to talk) but they certainly don't have the opportunity to work out an issue. Because that takes time and we are tired and just don't have the emotional energy to work through an issue.

If you find yourself in this situation you are in for a fall. It will not be pretty. If you want to avoid a catastrophe in the relationship – MAKE TIME! Book it in. Do not delay or you will pay. Do it now! Yup, I mean right now if you are long overdue for a talk. Just put the book down, walk over to your wife (or phone or email or text), and say, "We need to talk. Now would be good for me, but if not for you, let's set a time."

The truth is it's not about time. It's about priorities. You need to put having a good relationship high on your priority list. When it is a priority the time will be there. I know you and your partner may believe that a healthy relationship is your top priority but I say, if you want to see what is your top priority look at what you are doing and where you spend your time. Oops, looks like work is a top priority, and bringing up the kids (even though there is no time to play catch with Johnny or take Suzy for a walk to the playground), and looking after the household, which leaves little time for the relationship. As I was reading what I just wrote, I thought, maybe I am being a little hard. Maybe it's not just about prioritizing, but about awareness. Maybe a good relationship is a priority but it has gotten lost in the *have to do list*. I have to go to work, I have to pick up the groceries, I have to take the kids to school, and I have to, blah, blah, blah. Therefore, becoming aware of what is happening to your relationship and then taking action is critical.

For this to work, it is imperative to move the needs of the relationship into the have to do list. As in, I have to go out once a week with my spouse with no kids. I gave this assignment to a couple in their late thirties with four kids. They hadn't gone on a date in almost twenty years. This one action has contributed greatly to their marriage staying together. They love it and are going out one evening every week like clockwork. I'm impressed and they are a lot happier. This is also a time where they get to communicate without disruptions (though they try to avoid home talk – not romantic).

Denial

This is a biggy. You may be thinking – what problem? OK, there is a problem . . . but it's hers. Denial, denial, and more denial. Why is it so hard for men to admit that there is a problem? Maybe it is because we know the problem is in an area in which we don't feel confident. It is in the emotional arena and that makes us squeamish. Hey, if I deny it long enough maybe it will go away. What's more likely to happen is that *she* is going to go away.

Sometimes, the issue is more than simple denial. Sometimes, the guy genuinely believes what he is saying and it is not just denial. I call it a *FRIKKIN' BIG BLIND SPOT*. He just can't see the effect of his behavior on his partner or other family members. If you are one of these guys you are in serious trouble. The only process I know that might work in this case is video or serious psychotherapy. And if you are in denial it's not likely that you are going to do therapy. That leaves us with video.

Video is brutal in its ability to expose behavior to someone with a blind spot. Your wife can tell you that you pick your nose, your mother can tell you that you pick your nose, I can tell you that you pick your nose, and you still won't believe it. But when you see it on video . . . it's hard to deny. And it is such a wonderful moment to watch the stunned look on his face as he says, "Oh my God, I do pick my nose!" You gotta love it. End of blind spot (a famous example of this is David Hasselhoff being videoed and put on You-tube while drunk and eating a hamburger on the floor – nothing like public humiliation to send you to rehab).

How long is this going to take?

Don't let this question stop you from continuing the work. Success does not come overnight. Sorry, but that's the truth for learning effective communication and in life. How fast the process takes depends on a couple of factors. One, how weak are your communication skills and two, how long have you been ineffective. Also, it is an ongoing process as you and your partner learn and grow throughout your lives.

The next part of the equation is asking yourself how much time you are willing to put into learning and changing. The more effort you put in the faster the results. Finally, persistence and consistency are important.

The best case scenario I have seen was a couple of weeks but count on three to six months of daily practice. Often clients get some quick results and then there is a dip as both partners have to integrate the changes being made. Habits die hard and it is important to create new healthy habits to replace those you are trying to eliminate. You will go two steps forward and one backward but keep going. Eventually you will get there.

That reminds me, none of this will work if your partner refuses to co-operate. She will need to work on her own issues and modify her responses as you change. If the two of you are actively involved on the process success will be achieved much faster.

Avoidance

Avoidance is not as bad as denial, you are one step up – you know you have a problem, but you are not willing or feel incapable of solving it. We do this because:

- we are afraid
- we don't believe we will succeed
- we will get emotional
- it's a lot of work.

What Are Your Reasons For Avoiding?

1. _____

2. _____

3. _____

Tiredness

When we are confronted emotionally we get tired. We don't even have to be confronted directly, just thinking about an upcoming "talk" with our spouse can make us want to go to sleep, or run away or make up a lame excuse as to why we are going to be late getting home tonight.

And sometimes we are physically tired. This is usually from work. Don't use it as an excuse to avoid the situation. I don't care how tired you are, if there was a fire in your house you would instantly have a ton of energy. Well, there is a fire in your relationship and if you don't get moving everything you have worked so hard for is going to burn to the ground.

Summary:

Emotion, yours and your partner's, will often be the biggest blocks to effective communication. First you must be able to identify what emotion you are having and then be able to express it in a manner that is understood by the listener. When you are having a strong emotion, remember to breathe, so that your body and mind don't go into freeze mode.

Once you are able to deal with your emotions then you can deal with the other side of the coin – her emotions. How does her emotional response affect your thinking process and feeling? Do you become guilt ridden, angry or protective?

When you dissect your emotional response in an argument your "buttons" become obvious. Most of these buttons were created when we were children and a few later in life through important learning experiences (e.g., our first date). Becoming aware of your buttons, attitudes and beliefs about women allows you to master your behavior and stop being a victim to your emotional reactions.

Other issues to consider include: the need to know, the need to problem solve, lack of understanding and habits. Dealing with any of these issues makes us uncomfortable. By knowing that we are prepared for what is involved we therefore don't need to hide away from these difficult feelings when they arise.

Other obstacles or excuses are a lack of time by being too busy and tiredness. It is a matter of defining our priorities so that we take or make the time to have a loving and effective relationship. Denial or avoidance of problems will eventually lead to an unhappy state of affairs and the dissolution of the relationship.

Chapter 13

WIN THE ARGUMENT LOSE THE RELATIONSHIP

A man lives by believing something:
not by debating and arguing about many things.

Thomas Carlyle

The Ego

I'm right! You're wrong! Let me list the ways in which my point of view is true and yours is ridiculous. Sound familiar? This is what we think or say when engaged with our significant other. Unfortunately, this approach does not make her feel significant – just the opposite. She feels belittled, talked down to and not taken seriously.

Why is it that we treat the most important person in our life so shabbily when we disagree with their position? Even if they are wrong, you would think we would be able to convey our argument with maturity and not like a whacked out punk on drugs. Oh, you do explain in a rational, controlled manner. It is she who gets whacked out and hysterical. Very interesting!

Let's back up a little and examine what happens when we are in an argument. First, guys have been brought up, or in psychological language – conditioned – to win. We like winning. It feels good and everyone likes a winner. However, winning at all costs can be problematic both in our intimate relationships and in the outside world. I will not get into a discussion on ethics here but I hope you get the point. Most of our experiences as boys in competition were with other boys. Competing with girls did not happen as often and was considered not totally fair as they were weaker physically and it just wasn't right to tackle a girl as hard as a boy. We were taught to treat them differently. They were not as tough as us in our rough and tumble world. Besides, they were often happy to be playing their girl games which did not interest us in the least (at least not most of us).

We boys, who are now men, grew up competing with each other and we practiced winning. Even in conversation it was who is the smartest, who knows the most, and who had the smartest, quickest, funniest retort. We were constantly trying to outdo one another. This was even fun for some of us. We learned to admire those who were good at something and learned how to let putdowns and taunts roll off us or to reply in kind. We learned our place in the pecking order and how to live and work with it.

In order to win an argument boys and men will do whatever it takes to win. There is a lot at stake for us. Prestige is garnered when an argument is won – in my eyes and in the eyes of those watching. Interactions between men are often about one-upmanship. Boys and men have been known to even make up facts in order to win an argument. I'm not kidding. Ask any man. I remember how shocked my partner was when I told her this. "Why would you do this?" she asked.

In a man's way of thinking, at least when arguing, it is up to the opponent to know his or her facts well enough to catch me in my confabulation. If they can't, they don't deserve to win. This is of course simple justification and rationalization for lying. The point is, winning, and our need to win, is felt by men as equivalent to survival itself. We hate to admit we are wrong. And we especially hate to admit it to women. Being wrong is like being weak or vulnerable. No man wants to be in a position where they can be taken advantage of. This is tough enough when engaged with another man but there are rules and processes that we have practiced since we were kids. We know the game. But losing to the "weaker sex" is shameful. Worse, women don't know the rules and can easily castrate their partner without even realizing it. Castration is not fun! So, we avoid it at all costs.

How bad can it get? Here is a personal story. One day I was having a fight with my ex-wife and I was wrong about something. I even admitted I was incorrect. She then asked for an apology. I was dumbfounded. I had admitted I was wrong – surely that was enough. No it wasn't. As we examined why it was so difficult for me to apologize (she is a clinical psychologist), I realized that I had never apologized to a woman. I was in my mid-thirties at the time. Amazing! I couldn't have been right all the time, yet here I was feeling like someone was pulling a tooth without anesthetic. Saying, "I'm sorry," made me feel sick to my stomach.

That is *fear in action* as our Ego tries to preserve itself. In truth, it takes a big man to be able to admit when he is wrong and still maintain his dignity. Truth does indeed hurt sometimes but it need not be a soul destroyer. Quite the opposite. It is an opportunity for growth.

In a sense, we have to let our ego suffer a little death. It is important to know that we can survive such a process, and indeed, become stronger and more capable of relating to others, especially our significant other. In order to do this we must:

Become *aware* of what's happening.

If you feel yourself going on automatic pilot when arguing this is a warning flag that "**it**" has got "**you.**" You are **not** in control. You turn off the autopilot by taking a big breath, stop talking, re-collect your thoughts, and if you are really brave – tell your partner you were on autopilot.

- This means you have to let go of trying to win the argument. You must make it more important to discover what is driving your thoughts and feelings – what is controlling you – rather than winning the argument.

- Identify the feelings you are having. Am I angry, sad, suspicious, or confused? Whatever it is, identify it to yourself and to your partner.

When you take these steps the conversation becomes grounded in reality. This is what is really happening. The points are unimportant. What you are truly feeling and thinking is important.

- Discuss what is happening. Here's an example: "Honey, when you said that we had to go shopping right away, I got angry and felt like you were ordering me like my mother used to. I felt like I was ten years old and you had no regard for my feelings or what I was doing (like watching the last minute of a tie football, hockey or baseball game).

Now, she might have something to say to this. That's fine; at least you are talking about your experience. With luck she will be too. This way, your real concerns can be addressed in a mature manner instead of screaming at or ignoring her, which only leads to resentment and payback (e.g., putdowns, sarcastic remarks, no sex).

- Keep the goal in sight. What is it you are trying to achieve? It should be understanding, learning, appreciation, growing, peace and love. When you feel like killing the other you are on the wrong track. However, that urge is giving you information. Information as to what are your hot buttons. If you have a hot button, and we all do, this is an opportunity to explore. Put on your hiking boots and head into the jungle of your psyche.

Special note: *If you are too emotional for your own good, it may be necessary to remove yourself from the immediate environment until you have collected yourself enough to continue the discussion. Punching the wall (hurting self) or your partner is unacceptable and never improves a relationship. It is simply a demonstration of how helpless you feel (unless used deliberately to intimidate or coerce which is not recommended either if you want a healthy relationship).*

Acknowledging what is

This is a tricky process. Acknowledging *what is* means identifying what you are thinking, feeling, and even deeper than that, what is really driving your behavior. We are not initially conscious of these forces. It takes stopping what is happening and looking inward. You contemplate what has just happened in the past 60 seconds, how your body feels, identify what buttons were pushed, how you reacted (your behavior), and what were the origins of those sensitivities. This is no easy feat. To get a handle on this process in a real life situation you must:

1) Stop everything the moment you realize that you are in reaction mode

2) Tell your partner that you have just realized you are reacting

3) Apologize immediately if you have been a dork

4) Identify with her what you are really feeling (e.g., insecurity, fear, overwhelm)

5) If you can't identify what is happening ask her for assistance:

   - this might mean going over the past minute or so of the conversation and identifying the precise moment when you reacted and what was happening or being said
   - looking at past times where the same thing has happened
   - seeing if there are similar reactions with other people (look to close relationships like parents or siblings)
   - keep identifying and sharing your feelings as they change. For example, you may be embarrassed as you dig into your reactions and realize that your outburst had nothing to do with your wife but triggered an old incident with a previous girlfriend. As you share your uncomfortable feeling, this hopefully elicits caring, compassion, and support from your partner and will further the relationship and self-exploration.

This process can be extremely uncomfortable as we feel that we are in a vulnerable position. Being vulnerable is unpleasant for men as it can invite attack and no man wants to be caught with his drawers around his knees. Therefore, do not do this unless you and your spouse have an agreement not to attack the other when being vulnerable. Deep and effective communication cannot occur if there is no trust or safety.

TIP: *Have this conversation ASAP where you create a prearranged signal to remind the other person when they get lost in their stuff and forget loving action. The signal should be as outrageous as possible to immediately bring your partner to their senses.*

Having said that, depending on where the relationship is you may be starting in the hole where there is no trust or safety. Don't use this as an excuse not to try this process. Set up mutually agreeable ground rules and follow them to the best of your ability. With practice you will get better.

Letting go

The only constant is change. In order to grow as a person and in your relationship you must be willing to let go of old attitudes, beliefs and ways of behaving, and learn to embrace new understandings of yourself and your partner. In order to improve your communication you must peer into your feelings and examine what is driving them.

Letting go is easier if you tell yourself that changing your mind or your position is not losing. You are not losing when you are growing. You are not losing when you come to new understandings about yourself and your partner. And you are definitely not losing when you get more sex.

Keeping the goal in sight

What is the goal to keep in sight? At the simple level, more sex. Up one step is better communication. Up another level is a more loving relationship. Up another level is improved health and a greater sense of well-being through an enhanced relationship with your wife or partner. I say, use whatever works for you. Also, identify a goal or goals and remind yourself of them daily. The most effective time to remind yourself of your goal is right before it is about to be challenged. If you are about to have a discussion with your partner that you know is sensitive to you or to her – remind yourself of your goals and vision for the relationship. You may even want to remind her as well – not about the more sex goal though. Remind her of a goal that is important to her, unless, as my wife has just reminded me, you both share the same goal around sex.

The bottom line is that the overarching goal is more important than winning the argument. Winning the battle and losing the war is expensive both emotionally and financially.

Noticing the process

Noticing the process is difficult but possible. The reason for noticing the process is to make mid-course corrections when arguing or discussing or even reacting when listening to someone else's conversation. If you are able to identify when you slip into a reactive state, you can STOP. You can then take a few moments, or longer, to work out what happened, either in your own mind, or even better, with your partner. Then you can resume the discussion. Without this ability you are like a rocket without a guid- ance system. Who knows where it will land?

Admitting what's happened

Tell the truth. I know, this can be difficult, but hey, you are a big boy now and you will survive whatever she dishes out even if it feels like hell. It is impossible to have a healthy relationship based on lies. It doesn't work. Women can smell a rat a mile away and even if you are able to conceal a whopper, you have to remember what you said. Women remember what they have said – guys don't. So, who are you kidding? Save yourself a lot of time and energy and deal with reality. Tell the truth. Yes, I went to the bar with the guys for a couple (OK four) hours after work tonight.

Will she be upset? You bet. Especially if you didn't phone (Always phone. It is common courtesy and shows respect for the other person). Oh, you phoned but said you were working late and she found out anyway. Imagine a buzzer sound here. Wrong. Now you're being sneaky and a liar (but at least you made the phone call).

You can see how this becomes one big complicated mess. By admitting what you did upfront you shorten the whole discussion by an hour or two. You get right to her being pissed off with you. You were going there anyway so don't avoid it. Fess up. By stating the truth up front, not only do you shorten the process but you actually score a subtle point here. You show her you are willing to be honest. That demonstrates strength of character – impressive. It shows you are not a little weasel but a man who is willing to be accountable for his actions.

By simply admitting what happened you are rising in her estimation. Yes, you will have to weather the justifiable anger she will throw your way, but you lied, and now you have to eat it. Be humble, admit your mistake and figure out how to make up for it. Oh, and don't do it again. This shows that you are capable of learning. This is important because you will make mistakes, but now she knows you can learn and she will be more willing to trust you are not coming from a bad place. There is nothing worse than going over the same mistake again and again. It erodes the relationship and destroys hope.

Starting over and backtracking

This is a continuation of the concept of admitting what's happened. In other words, it's never too late to say, "Honey, I realized that I have been

_____." This could be lying, stonewalling, talking off

topic, reacting, fooling yourself – whatever. The longer you wait to state the truth of your experience the harder it is to admit. *You become invested in the reactive defense system you are creating.* The only way to break through is to tell the truth.

Dealing with vulnerability

Vulnerability. The word that can make a grown man cringe in fear. Why on earth would you make yourself vulnerable? It is like going into battle and the enemy says, "Hey, why don't you drop your sword and shield and let's talk?" Yeah right! The most you might get from a guy in this situation is, "You first." Yet, in an intimate relationship this is exactly what must be done – dropping your guard and letting go of your weapons.

To help in the effort tell yourself:

1) She is not the enemy even though every cell in your body is screaming to run or attack
2) War doesn't solve problems; it just makes you feel good in the moment
3) The sooner you start talking the sooner you will have peace. And with peace comes all sorts of benefits.

Vulnerability is not about being defenseless. It is about being open and honest. It is about identifying your thoughts and feelings and *sharing* them. Sharing feelings can be tough when there is so much crap in the way. There is the macho image about men and feelings which just messes everything up when it comes to communication and relationship.

Yes, it does feel like you are naked and in front of an audience when you first learn to put your weapons down (e.g., sarcasm, silence, shouting) and truly listen and then respond with your experience in a non-combative manner. You will be awkward – fumbling for words – and trying to understand what is happening to you. And then there is your partner's experience to take into consideration as well. This can make your head spin.

The good news is that the more you do it the better you get and, somewhere in the process, you realize that you can be vulnerable and still protect yourself if the other person attacks. Yes. It does happen as you know all too well. Sometimes you do put the shield down and they attack. It does happen.

Creating a safe space

If your home has become a battle ground you will need to create a demilitarized zone (DMZ). The DMZ is a place in the house that is neutral ground where you and your partner go to work things out; or it could be the head space you and your partner need to get into before talking. Ideally, it is both and, at a minimum, it is the mental space you get into to prepare yourself before engaging with each other.

What does it take to create a safe place or DMZ? First, both people have to agree to it. If you are going to create a safe place in the house in which to have your important discussions, you both have to agree where that is. Once you agree on the borders (the den for example) the rules that govern the space need to be set. No physical or verbal violence is a typical requirement. In other words, no hitting, swearing or character assassination within the borders of the DMZ even when engaged in a difficult and heated exchange (this should be true outside the DMZ as well but, if not, the DMZ is a good place to start).

What you are trying to create is a space where you can freely exchange your thoughts and feelings without fear of being attacked. To do this you must take responsibility for the words that come out of your mouth and the actions you take with your body (no physical harm or aggression to self or other).

If you choose not to have an actual area for the DMZ you can create the space any time and any place. Again, the rules that govern this psychological space must be determined before the fight, sorry, "discussion", begins. Have a conversation with your partner when you are both in good moods and discuss the way you want to be and the rules that will support you when under stress and needing to have a conversation.

There are two areas I have been alluding to above – physical safety and emotional safety. Both must be taken into account when creating a safe space.

TIP: *Before beginning the conversation tell your partner that you love her even though you are upset and need to talk to her. This works much better than opening with a threat like, "If you don't change, I'm leaving."*

Boundaries

Simply put, if you get angry or disturbed by someone thinking or acting differently than you, and insist that they change, you have a boundary issue at a minimum. You may have more serious psychological problems as well. If you try to physically make someone do something you have crossed the line into trying to control their behavior. Your partner is an independent person with her own thoughts and feelings. They may not always match yours. This is OK. If it is a threat to you this is an indication that something within you is being challenged and needs to be examined.

This approach does not justify all thinking or behavior. If your partner thinks it is OK to have an affair and you don't, then you definitely have the right to state your boundaries and the consequences if they are broken (e.g., you will leave the relationship). Obviously, a discussion before becoming partners should have occurred in which the two of you identify key beliefs, desires, goals and ways of being so that it is clear what is acceptable and what isn't. Unfortunately, this discussion rarely happens.

Asking for help

Another challenge to the ego is *asking for help*. Again, it is the myth of being totally self-sufficient that we are battling here. Heck, even the Lone Ranger had help. Asking for help means we need someone else. This puts you in a position of vulnerability and being one-down. This is a double whammy. And finally, we may even have to accept someone else's suggestion. Horror of horrors!!! We could not figure it out by ourselves. "What is wrong with me? Can't I stand on my own two feet? I am not strong and capable." These are disabling thoughts that keep us from getting the help we need.

In order to reframe the situation think like a business person. Would you hire an accountant to do the company taxes? Of course! Would you hire an architectural engineer to design the new plant? Of course you would. So why not ask for help in your personal life. Think efficiency and successful goal attainment and stop worrying about how you look to others. Be smart and get results. Talk to a friend, your partner or a professional. Do whatever it takes to ensure the success of your marriage and your well-being.

Hearing the help

Great! You have asked for help. Now comes an even bigger challenge. Hearing it! You see, our ego is so big it will not want to entertain a suggestion that is different from what it already knows. It thinks – everyone else is crazy. Why don't they do it my way? The ego will get stubborn, resistant and even throw a tantrum. *Why did this have to happen to me? You can't trust anyone these days.* It will consume more drugs or alcohol to avoid dealing with the issue or use the addiction as an excuse for lack of action. It will become abusive to others in an attempt to drive them away rather than deal with the problem. Our egos are problem avoiders. Remember, the ego sees change as death. So, of course it will do anything to avoid change. Who wants to die?

You, on the other hand, will need to take control. You will have to tell that panicked ego that change is the way to success even if it feels like death. The ego will need to expand in order to incorporate new information and practice new behaviors which will ultimately lead to a new way of thinking about self and the world. This is what the ego fears. It fears this change. It fears change because it is unpredictable. As the old saying goes, "Better the devil you know rather than the one you don't." That is how the ego thinks.

You took the big step of asking for help so why not try to hear what is being said. Yes, it may contradict what and how you think about life, or how your partner should behave, but doing it the old way is what got you into the problem in the first place. If you knew what to do to solve the problem you would have done it. In order to hear, you will need to be brutally honest with yourself. As you can see, the real argument is not with your spouse but with your ego, and your ego is a thousand times trickier than your spouse.

Summary:

Learning to keep the real goal in sight is critical to a healthy relationship and learning to communicate effectively. The real goal is a better relationship (which means more sex) not winning an argument (which means less sex). Unfortunately, it is not just this simple otherwise we could just forfeit all arguments and have lots of sex. No, that won't work. Like in any game that is deliberately lost all the time, no one wants to play with you. People aren't stupid and neither is your partner. They will see through the ruse.

You have to step up to the plate and learn how to face major league pitches. This takes guts when you see the ball (her anger, disappointment, complaint) come hurtling at you at over a hundred miles an hour. Your ego will want to duck out of there as fast as possible. It is an act of will to stay firmly planted in the batter's box.

What will help you stay in the game is to know that you were brought up to compete. Unfortunately, many of us were taught that losing was shameful. This is ridiculous, as losing is a part of life and learning how to lose gracefully seems to be a lost art. It has been so ingrained in us that losing feels like death that our ego will do anything to avoid losing. It becomes blinkered and cannot see anything other than what is straight in front of it. It only wants to win and will do whatever it takes to win even hurting the relationship. The ego is that fearful and insecure.

You must become aware of what is happening to you in the moment by identifying your thoughts and feelings and then be willing to discuss them with your partner while always keeping the true goal in sight. In the process you will become aware of useless attitudes and beliefs and learn to let go of outdated programming. Constant upgrading ensures smooth operations.

Telling the truth about what is happening may be diffi-cult and facing her reaction can be fearsome (or disappointing or _____ fill in the blank) but is essential to creat-ing a safe and trusting space where growth and change can occur. Learn-ing to respect boundaries, yours and hers, enhances the feeling of safety.

Finally, if things get a little crazy, be willing to ask for help and then listen and act on the advice. You don't have to do it all by yourself, as that is another useless myth we have swallowed whole and it will choke us to death.

Chapter 14

HOW TO MAINTAIN A HEALTHY CAR...
I MEAN RELATIONSHIP

Piglet sidled up to Pooh from behind.
"Pooh!" he whispered. "Yes, Piglet?"
"Nothing," said Piglet, taking Pooh's paw.
"I Just wanted to be sure of you".

A. A. Milne

Love is <u>not</u> enough

All you need is love. Unfortunately, the Beatles and countless modern and ancient poets were wrong. Love is great but it will not, nor should it, keep an abusive partnership together. More often than not it does keep the relationship together and with disastrous results. I have seen it many times amongst my friends, with clients, and in my own life.

That feeling of love is so indefinable yet we crave it and are intoxicated by it. I remember someone saying that falling in love is Nature's way of hooking up men and women long enough so that they procreate because without that feeling we would rather live with those of the same sex. He had a point, and many cultures had this figured out ages ago. Marriage was seen as the joining together of families. It was a financial arrangement. Love was not the issue and was seen as problematic, if it arose at all.

What is love? First, it is a feeling. When we think of our beloved whom we have known for one second (love at first sight) or many years, we have a desire to embrace them. To take them in our arms and merge.

To become one with them. Our hearts beat faster, our skin seems more sensitive, our breathing changes. We feel happy, excited, even drunk.

Love can be visualized along a continuum with infatuation at one end and what I call deep love at the other. Deep love is a rich love that has ripened like wine over the years. Its bouquet has many overtones and the taste lingers on the palette long after the initial infusion. It is a love where one would sacrifice oneself willingly for the other. This is a love born over time unlike the love for a child which can be instantaneous.

Love is action

But I love her. Really? What do you do to show your love? Well, she knows I love her. How? Do you tell her . . . regularly? As in, at least once a week. What about flowers? What about them you ask? Women love flowers (at least most of them do. I have met one that didn't. If you are going out with that one in a thousand – find a substitute. For the flowers, not the woman!).

In this crazy rush-rush world of work and driving the kids to all the events they belong to it is easy to get out of the behaviors you and your partner used to do to show love and affection for each other. We start to take the other for granted over time, slowly but surely, they become like a good friend (if you are lucky) or like your mother (if you are unlucky). Either way, it takes the edge off the sex drive – at least with that person. If you are loyal you chalk it up to the demands of work and modern life. If you aren't – you fool around.

The trick is to not let it get to this state and if it does, to intervene as soon as possible. I have worked with many couples that benefited from instituting a ritual of going out on a date once a week (without the kids) even after 15 years of not doing it. Women love being treated in a special way. It reminds them that you see them as a special person and not just as the cook or homemaker or the mother to your kids or another paycheck (working partners).

"But I'm not a romantic guy" you say. Who cares! Do you want a happy relationship or no? Fake it. She will appreciate it even more. Because she is not stupid! She knows you hate the romantic stuff. And yet you have dressed up, picked out a nice restaurant and bought a rose in her favourite color no less. You have gone to all this trouble for her. She feels special beyond belief and you have scored so many brownie points it is ridiculous. To top it off, you take her dancing, and I am not kidding, EVEN IF YOU DON'T DANCE. Happy times are coming your way.

You see, it is crucial that you realize everyone, including your partner, wants to be loved. Not just told they are loved, but to experience the action of love. There is a difference between you feeling love, which you may, and her experiencing it. If you beat her every second day, you may love her but she will have a hard time believing it. Or as often happens, she may know you love her but be confused by your actions. This is an extreme case, I know, but it illustrates the point. Actions speak louder than words.

Some women like to be told that you love them. If you have trouble saying "I love you," it is time to figure out why. Either you don't love her or you have an issue. If you have an issue that is brought up by this phrase, seek professional help. If you don't love her and she thinks you are in a relationship that includes this concept you need to be honest with her.

Here's a little story to illustrate the point. I had a couple in counseling and their relationship was on the rocks. They had been together for 25 plus years and the woman had finally had it. He was only there because she had threatened to leave (as is often the case, she had asked him for years to come to counseling but he refused. Go the first time your wife brings it up even if it is the first year of a marriage). The wife felt completely ignored and I asked her if it would make a difference to get flowers from her husband. "I love flowers she replied" and "Yes, it would make a difference." The husband looked at me with disdain and said, "I hate flowers." I just about swatted him across the head as I said, "You're not buying them for you. You're buying them for her." He didn't get it. He thought because he didn't like flowers that his wife should have the same reality. Wake-up call guys. Not so! Women have an independent mind and if you don't acknowledge this you are in for some hard time in your relationship.

List time again. Write out a list of what you DO to show your wife you love her. Next write out a list of what your wife says she would like you to DO that demonstrates your love for her. Compare the lists and change accordingly. You want to do what she thinks demonstrates love. This can also be a great topic of conversation with her. You may be doing things that she is unaware of or places little value on. What you want to do is find the highest ROI (return on investment which in this case is your time and effort). You may be doing things that have no meaning for her and wondering why she wasn't appreciating your efforts but ignoring something that tells her absolutely that you love her. Find out what that thing is and life will get easier.

What I Do To Show Love

1) _____

2) _____

3) _____

4) _____

5) _____

What She Wants To Feel Loved

1) _____

2) _____

3) _____

4) _____

5) _____

When we first met

Do you remember the first time you met? What did you notice about her? What did you find attractive – her hands, her mouth, her breasts, her legs, her voice. What did you feel? Happy, nervous, scared, sexy, romantic, lustful, hopeful? What thoughts went through your head? Did you fantasize about the future or were you thinking how to get her into bed that night? Maybe you were just a kid and kissing was a big deal.

I remember the longest kiss I have ever had. I was eleven years old at the time and Christina (this is a miracle, I remember her first and last name. Normally my brain is a sieve when it comes to remembering names) and I were involved with a couple of other kids in a kissing contest. This was a joy as she and I had been eyeing each other for a while. One half hour – WOW! I was in heaven. That record still stands over forty years later. You might not think that half an hour is very long but to appreciate the feat it is important to know that I am asthmatic and my nose is often plugged. We were in a lip lock and the judges were on us to make sure there were no gaps in the seal.

Moving forward in time to my current partner, I remember the first time we met. In a sense, I met her for the first time twice. The first time I was married to someone else and we were introduced at a Christmas party. As we were shaking hands I got a jolt of electricity. It was an emotional hit of attraction/connection that scared the hell out of me. After all, I was newly married and loyal. I immediately let go of her hand and disappeared as fast as I could. Never saw her again – until ten years later.

I was now divorced and living in another city. It was Christmas time and I came back to visit family and friends. While out with a male friend he asked if I was looking for some action. I had been separated from my wife for a year and a half and had been happily celibate during that period. I was now ready to break out and have a good time. My friend asked me if there was anyone I would like to hook up with. I immediately answered with, "Paulette." Again, my-can't-remember-a-name-two-seconds-after-you-have-told-me brain recalled the name of a woman I met once, at a party, ten years ago. Amazing!

When we finally met a few days later I remember two things. One, she was older than I remembered (ten years had passed) and two, when she smiled . . . I was a goner. Her face lit up and my heart was jelly. We have been together ever since.

Why did I tell you these stories? To remind you of the fun, excitement and sometimes sheer terror of meeting your partner. It was alive. You were alive. The possibilities and dreams were endless. Is this your relationship today? Probably not. Can you recapture those feelings? I don't know. I am not sure if that is even a good thing. But, you can capture the spirit of that time. Those first days, weeks and months of a new relationship are heady times. And time changes our love. If you are lucky it evolves and deepens. I know from experience that the excitement can be recaptured. Maybe not at the same intensity or duration as those first six months to a year, but it is excitement and love for sure and, from my experience and that of others I have talked to, it is a much richer and deeper love.

Why do we stop doing what worked?

In the process of recapturing that excitement a question arises. Why did we stop doing what worked? You were polite, playful, thoughtful, bought little gifts and most of all – you were attentive. You listened and were helpful if it was needed.

Somehow, once the quarry has been captured and we refocus on work, we make the assumption that our partner does not need any maintenance. Wrong! Granted, you may not be able to be as attentive, but like your favourite car, regular maintenance is the guarantee to a long lasting and satisfying relationship whether it is with your car or your wife.

What is regular maintenance for your partner? It is probably some variation of what worked when you first got together. Maybe you went dancing, took long walks, went to the movies, made dinner, played cards, bought flowers, left love notes . . . you get the idea. If you are not sure what makes your wife feel appreciated and looked after – ask. And then make a list (this may be the same as the previous list only expanded).

Make sure that you have at least ten items recorded and pick at least one per week. I keep the list pinned to the wall in front of my computer. That way it is a constant reminder and a handy resource.

Love is like a car. Good maintenance = Good performance and longevity

Now back to our car analogy (or any item or activity that you lavish attention on. It could be your coin collection, motorcycle, or curling). As the heading above states, good and consistent maintenance leads to a long and happy relationship. You wouldn't dream of not putting oil in the motor of your car and yet you forget to bring flowers to your partner. Things like hugs, love notes, saying "I love you," flowers or meals out are the oil of the relationship. It demonstrates that you are thinking and doing something for the relationship. Women really, really like this and will show their appreciation. Likewise if you don't do proper maintenance things will get rough and noisy just like an engine without oil. Eventually there will be a big explosion and the car/relationship will be broken, finished, kaput. It is a rather sickening noise and feeling when the relationship blows. I don't recommend it.

And like a car that has been bought on time, you will have payments even after it has fallen apart. Paying for something that is not there really sucks. And it can all be avoided by a simple and regular maintenance plan. Pay a little now or pay big later. It's up to you.

Spark plugs = Romance

Most women love romance. Most guys I know (except for the French and Italian ones – I'm stereotyping for effect here. I know there are romantic men in all cultures) are lukewarm at best. For a woman, romance is their way of knowing that you care. That you care enough to buy flowers, plan a meal out, pick a movie that she likes, dress up and generally make her feel like a queen. It goes to the heart of all their fantasies. You are the knight in shining armor. The best part is that you don't have to look the part. Your girlfriend/wife is very accepting of how you look. She would not have picked you if she wasn't. Just know that all you have to do is invest some time and effort in playing out the part.

Again, it is really not difficult but it does take time. Hell, if you have the money you can have your assistant figure out all the details and make the arrangements. If you are not in that category you will have to do it yourself. Research is the key in this endeavor. If you do not already know, find out her favorite restaurant or food and what kind of entertainment she likes. Does she like dancing, going for a drive, watching the sun set? You can do one activity or combine a number of activities. And don't forget chocolate. A survey showed that women like chocolate even more than sex. I say combine the two and then you have a win/win situation.

If you have a knack for romance or want to take it up a notch you can get creative. My French-Canadian friend once set a trail of notes that took his beloved on a treasure hunt around the city and eventually to him sitting in a restaurant waiting for her with a major gift. A simpler version is leaving hidden love notes which she will find when she opens a drawer or computer. This is both a surprise and a reminder that you are thinking loving thoughts about her. Women love this stuff.

Spring tune-up = Vacation

There is nothing like a vacation to tune up the relationship. You get to see each other in a new light as you scrape off last year's grime that has accumulated under the hood of the car/relationship. Going away presents the opportunity to relate with each other without the pressures of every-day life stressing you out. With less stress comes a resurgence of sexual energy. You heard me. A woman who is stress free is relaxed and a relaxed woman is able to invite you in with much more ease. The vacation is like a car getting all lubed up. There is a lot less friction and all parts are greased and working with ease. In essence, the vacation can add new spark plugs to the relationship. All cylinders are firing and the timing is spot on. The engine is purring and receptive to the slightest pressure on the gas pedal. I don't know about you but this is getting me excited!

You don't have to be rich to do this. Camping trips work just as well as vacations to tropical paradises. My partner and I just went on the best camping trip of my life and had a wonderful time. I have camped throughout my life and now in my late-fifties I just had the best camping experience ever. Who could have predicted that?

The vacation demonstrates to your wife that you consider her an important asset. Not only that, but you consider yourself worthy of a vacation. Women like men who take care of themselves. The woman in your life feels that she will be taken care of and respected. A woman who feels cherished (like your 67 Mustang) will perform accordingly. Going out for a drive will be a rewarding experience for the both of you.

Don't forget the basics. The spring tune-up involves changing the tires. In a relationship this can be related to a new wardrobe. If your wife has her own money make sure to remind her to take the time for spring shopping. That will really blow her mind and make the evening fun as she gives you a fashion show – clothes on, clothes off, her smiling as you show your appreciation at how wonderful she looks. Tough job but somebody has to do it and it might as well be you rather than her girlfriend. If it is your money either go with her (if you can stomach this you will be a superhero) or give her the money and say, "surprise me." You can't lose. One last thing, don't forget to update your wardrobe as well.

Grease = Flowers + Time

It's the little things that over time make the difference between a successful relationship and one bogged down in misery. Regular maintenance is crucial. Don't buy flowers once a year on Mother's day. Buy them every week (every second week at a minimum. If you can't afford it pick them when in season or find a cheaper alternative). Don't go out for a meal just on your anniversary but go out as much as you can afford it. My wife (and we eat out a lot) loves it every single time that we go out and I pay the bill. She just smiles and talks to me like I have just slain a dragon.

I know it is a nice thing I have done but she is responding from a primal place and this response is activated to a larger degree than you or I would be on a night out. This means something to her. I know it (though I may not understand why) and I will keep doing it because I enjoy a stress free relationship and like making love. This is not rocket science gentlemen. Do what works and leave the complaining for the guys who are not getting any loving.

Tire Pressure = Smooth riding (keeping the pressure just right)

Keeping your tires inflated at the right pressure improves the gas mileage and reduces wear and tear on the tires. What part of the relationship is represented by the tires? What keeps your relationship rolling along with minimal effort? It is the ongoing application of all the above items we have been discussing. It is a lot harder and takes more energy to move a vehicle from a standing start than to keep a moving vehicle rolling along. So, don't get behind. Keep a steady application of vehicle maintenance and loving care and you will be rewarded in kind.

Car wash = Showing you value what you have

A man who washes his car and keeps it looking shiny is someone who values what he has. I am not suggesting that you wash your wife (though that can be fun too) but do things that show your appreciation of her. Just as you like to accessorize your car your wife will appreciate any accessories you buy for her or make positive comments on the accessories that she buys for herself. We wash our car so that it looks good. Same with your wife. Anything that makes her look (or feel) good will get you bonus points. So spruce up those compliments and/or open up your wallet.

Fender Benders. Repairing hurts and mistakes . . . accidents happen

Accidents happen, what can I say? We yell, or get moody, or make a hurtful comment. You are not perfect, nobody is. What to do? First apologize as soon as you realize what has happened. If you don't, the hurt is like rust on your car. If not dealt with quickly it eats away at the body. If not attended to corrosion can hide under the paint and spread. Everything looks normal until one day the fender falls off, or worse. Don't delay on this one guys. There is nothing worse than a woman who has become bitter and is seeking revenge. The cost of repair can be prohibitive and many times the car/relationship is unsalvageable.

The best way to make sure rust is not getting under the paint is to have weekly visual checks. In a relationship this means taking the time to talk and ask how your wife is feeling. How is she feeling generally and specifically about the relationship? Are you and she in synch? Have you said or done anything that has upset her? This is a great maintenance program as it is proactive and you will be able to clean up any bumps, dents, scratches or rust at the early stages and with little effort (unless you did something really stupid in which case there will be need for major repairs).

Major Accidents

You just had to have an affair. Or you forgot the anniversary or the birthday. Or you were entranced with a beautiful young woman at a party and forgot that you came with your wife. Or even worse, you have been ignoring her throughout the week. Whatever you do, don't ignore her. Everything else is repairable.

Let's start with the worst case scenario – an affair. I will assume that there is no emotional attachment and that you want to stay married. The easiest way out of this problem is to never have it. Have a conversation with your wife at the beginning of your relationship where you both agree on monogamy (and if you agree on an open relationship this won't be a problem – so they say) and state that if ever either one of you want to have sex with someone else you come to your partner first to discuss it before acting on the need.

This does two things. If you or she wants to have an affair it is indicative that there is a problem in the relationship or it may be just a biological urge. Either way the choice to have an affair or not is yours to make and by talking to her you will have the opportunity to address it. It is a difficult situation but it is a preemptive action you are taking and trying to fix it after an affair is much more difficult if not impossible.

Second, you will have stayed true to your word which promotes trust (the affair destroys trust) and both partners will be intact. What I mean by this is that you will have seriously damaged if not destroyed the safety and uniqueness of the relationship by having an affair. The hurt is immense and the consequences are huge. The marriage is shattered, any trust is lost, your kids will freak out and now you have a real life enemy. To paraphrase Congreve, an English poet and playwright, hell hath no fury like a woman scorned. So, if you want to enter hell – have an affair.

Oh, I almost forgot. Divorces are expensive.

I can hear you thinking. *But talking about wanting to have an affair is not easy.* NO SHIT! Especially as many guys would love to be sleeping with a different woman every day. Do not be confused with your everyday testosterone level drive for sex and really, really wanting to have an affair because you and your partner have become disconnected whether emotionally or physically. Whether you think you have fallen in love/lust with someone else or you haven't had sex with your partner for three months after the birth of your child you need to honor her and yourself and have a talk. If you are smart this talk will happen as soon as you realize that something is up (no pun intended) and not when it is too late (after you have slept with someone).

Insurance paid annually = renew your vows, taking stock, visioning

Yes, you can take out a kind of insurance on your relationship. It ranges from the romantic (renewing your vows) to the practical (quarterly meeting to assess the state of the union). This is a time to assess and make new commitments to improve the relationship. Even the act of meeting demonstrates to your partner your commitment to her and the relationship. If things are not so good it is time to either put a recovery plan in place or get help. If things are good you can identify what is working and then go out and celebrate.

For those of you who have had, or are in a long term relationship, you know how busy life is. What with work, the kids, and all the family activities it is easy to be in survival mode and your most important relationship gets the short end of the stick. That is why it is so important to plan time to be together and to work on the relationship. If you don't, one day you will wake up and realize you have a blown motor, the gears have seized up and the rear end is shot. Not a pleasant experience I can assure you.

Appreciating assets. Antiques looked after go up in value

The great thing about a long term successful relationship is that like an antique car it goes up in value and you appreciate it more and more every year. You love to keep it in tip top shape, taking it out for a spin and showing it off to admiring friends. Your love and appreciation is obvious as you pamper your vehicle and talk about it in glowing terms to anyone who will listen. It is the same with your wife.

When you have invested time and energy in the relationship – taken care of it through the years – the relationship deepens and positively glows with health. This sort of relationship is not an accident. It is the result of care and attention.

Note: *Please don't tell your wife I called her an antique. We'll both be in trouble.*

Running out of gas = Taking your eye off the ball

Have you ever run out of gas? Embarrassing isn't it? Were you trying to save some money or just push it to see if you could make it without filling up?

What was your lesson learned from running out of gas? Mine was to look into the future, just a little and head off a problem before it happened. Heck, there is even a gauge to tell you, "Warning, you are about to run out of gas and life is about to become inconvenient." And yet, even with a gauge, people run out of gas all the time. Don't engage in self-sabotaging behavior. Pay attention to the warning signs in your relationship. This is so important we are going to do a list again.

Warning Signs List

Example: We are fighting more than usual. She hasn't talked to you for two days. The last three meals have been burnt. She is not cooking at all. Sex . . . what's that? Every couple has their very specific warning signs. If you are not sure what they are consult with your partner.

<u>Warning Signs</u>

1) _____

2) _____

3) _____

Summary:

Like maintaining a car, maintaining a relationship takes time and attention. Just admiring your car (or wife) doesn't do anything for its well-being. You have to roll up your sleeves, get some hot water and soap and start scrubbing. Heck, this could be fun.

A little bit of care and attention on a regular basis will pay off over the years as the object of your love reflects back to you the love you have lavished upon her. Love is action and love by itself does not make a relationship or guarantee effective communication. People don't want to just hear that you love them they want to experience it. Actions speak louder than words (but remember to speak the words as well if this is important to her).

To make sure we know what actions to take you created two lists (and if you didn't, do it now) – a list of what you currently do to show her that you love her and a list of what she wants you to do so that she feels loved.

Thinking back to when you first met your partner and remembering the feelings and activities you used to do together can help you get back in touch with both how you felt and what worked in the relationship. We tend to stop doing what worked once we are secure in the relationship – mistake!

Regular maintenance, like getting her flowers, taking her out to the movies, or dinners, go a long way to lubricating the engine of love. Learning how to be romantic is the spark that turns the engine over. Romance requires a bit of forethought because it is not natural to most guys. And yet there is usually one guy we know who has this skill. Consult with him or do some research or ask your wife what she finds romantic.

At least once or twice a year you take the car in for a major tune up. Likewise, a vacation is an opportunity to take the time to re-energize the relationship and buff out all the dings and scratches that have accumulated over the year. If you can afford it, the more vacations the better. These need not be expensive. They could be week-end getaways, camping trips or even staycations. Again, making it happen will be greatly appreciated.

In the same way you like to buy accessories for your car or favorite hobby, your wife likes to be accessorized as well. Gifts are appreciated at any time and are the equivalent to shop repairs when a fender-bender (a hurt) has occurred. If it is a major accident it will require major repairs. The bigger the accident the bigger the bill. Therefore, avoid reckless behavior and for God's sake don't have an affair. It's usually a total write off.

Chapter 15

THE BIG PICTURE

The quality of your life is the quality of your relationships.
Anthony Robbins

The Successful Relationship Formula

There is the short answer and the long answer in describing the formula for success in a relationship. The short answer is: buy a rubber doll. You can use her when you want, she doesn't talk back or nag, maintenance costs are minimal, and when the relationship stops working there are no divorce costs. What could be better?

Oh, you actually want someone to talk to. You want someone who gives you love and affection. You want someone to share your dreams with. You want someone to . . . you fill in the blanks. Even make a list if you care to of what you want out of a relationship. Oh, we did that already. If you haven't done it this is another chance.

Being clear on what you want will determine the type of person you will need to look for. If you are a traditionalist you will have to find a like-minded person if you want success. Don't go after a high-powered business woman if you want a stay at home Mom and three kids. On the other hand, if you want to stay home and look after the kids, that high-powered business woman might be perfect for you.

The relationship success formula looks like this. Ingredients: two people who are willing and able to communicate and through their communication come to resolutions that are mutually satisfying to both partners (think win/win). Notice that I said two people. You can learn all the communication skills in the world but if your partner is unwilling or unable to communicate, is a control freak, or hates your guts – it will not work. Not now, not ever. Get out and find someone else.

There are two aspects to consider in the successful relationship formula: communication skills and personality. We have not talked a lot about personality so let's briefly explore this aspect. Everyone is different but there are types. We know this instinctively and philosophers and psychologists are fascinated with personality. Why? If we understand people we can better predict their behavior. I want to know beforehand whether this woman is the type who will stab me in the middle of the night or throw dishes or get along with my parents, or at least make the attempt.

Being able to predict behavior is valuable on many levels. Unfortunately, men tend to get so focused on the pursuit, or blinded by women's beauty, or thinking with that small brain between our legs, that we are in a state of diminished capacity to make sound judgments on her personality. This process is made even more difficult because the other person is on their best behavior and trying like mad to hide any faults (we do this too, that is if we admit to any faults).

This idea of matching up personalities can be seen in astrology – are we good signs for each other, numerous other esoteric beliefs, matchmakers, and in psychology. Psychology doesn't advertise itself as a matchmaking service but it has created personality inventories to match up people with careers, workers with jobs, and people for teams. If you check out dating sites they have their own tests to try and match people by personality. The problem is, not whether these tests work or not, many are highly effective at what they say they will do, but even when you hook up with a compatible personality, do both of you have the communication skills to make it work?

What is a compatible personality? There is no empirically validated test that I know of for this question. There is the old adage that opposites attract but research shows that people who are more similar often stay together [46, 47]. You on the other hand probably have a pretty good idea of what kind of personality you like. The big question is . . . is what you like good for you?

If you go out with a stripper (no offence meant but there are a number of behaviors and situations that are common to this group) and then are surprised she does drugs, has a lot of old boyfriends hanging around, and keeps odd hours . . . wake up buddy! Contra-wise, if you go out with a regular church-going woman who wears long sleeves and high collars all the time, don't be surprised that she goes to bed at nine and wears flannel PJs (I'm exaggerating for effect here. I am sure there are lots of hot church-going-women out there – flannel will do that).

The point is that you need to know yourself. If you are unaware or don't care, you are probably one of those men I see in my office. They are confused and depressed that the women in their lives are angry or have left them. Don't be one of these men, please. Do yourself a favour and learn about yourself. Become conscious of what motivates you to act as you do. This will make change in your life easier and will make you much more attractive to the opposite sex and even your wife.

Have you ever met, cross that out; have you ever *lived* with a woman who is easy to get along with? I can see your eyes rolling upwards. I know,

I know, they are sooo demanding, and picky and moody. But, maybe they are that way for a reason and *you* may be that reason. Find out. It could be the first step to a much more pleasant experience.

For the sake of argument, let's say you are a reasonable, intelligent and caring kind of guy. We'll even add in humorous, as surveys tell us that humor rates high on women's lists of attributes they like in men [48]. What kind of personality should you consider for success? Easy-going! But I thought there were no easy-going women out there. Newsflash! There are, even if rare. Maybe the reason they are so rare is that they have to put up with a lot of unaware guys who don't know how to communicate. That's what I keep hearing from all these women.

However, even this is no guarantee. My ex-wife was easy going and it didn't work. I must have horseshoes up my butt as the next woman I met was also easy going. Being a little bit wiser this time I went for someone who was the same age as me (my first wife was 13 years younger). We have been together fourteen years and it gets better all the time. I am blessed and I know it. Do we have tiffs? Of course, but they don't last long and we use them to get closer with each other. I highly recommend easy going on the personality chart. But that is my need and it may not be yours. Remember, we are all unique and it is OK if you want a competitive high-energy over-achiever. You may need that kind of stimulation to keep your interest.

To sum up the Relationship Success Formula – find someone you respect who fits your personality and where you and she have good communication skills. If you have the same libido, or can negotiate a reasonable compromise, you have hit the jackpot. There is flex in this formula but any flex is dependent on your ability to communicate. If you want to know how to figure out sexual compatibility get my ebook The Sex Formula:

How to calculate sexual compatibility.

You can get it at www.**thesexformula**.com

Loving attention

There are other aspects of the relationship that can support success. One of these is loving attention. Loving attention is different from the efforts required for high maintenance women. What a high maintenance woman needs is a servant. Don't be a servant! You will eventually resent it.

Giving loving attention may or may not come naturally. If it doesn't come naturally you will have to plan for it. Remember the guy who didn't understand that buying flowers was what his wife wanted and not dependent on what he thought she should want. He was unable to grasp the concept that his wife was separate from him. If he did not like flowers he assumed that she didn't or shouldn't either.

As outrageous as this may sound, I have encountered this enmeshment between couples more times than I care to think about. It's depressing. Please remember, you are buying flowers for her, not for you. When you buy gifts it communicates to your wife you are thinking about her and putting out the time and effort to get something she likes. Women appreciate this and will love you for it.

Take time to talk

This may sound obvious but in our crazy world finding time to talk is difficult. Throw kids into the mix and the only time to talk is right before bed and that is when exhaustion takes over. Besides, I have to read a report and she wants to read her book. Many couples don't even go to bed at the same time. One of them is asleep when the other partner comes to bed. This is not conducive to talking or sex.

Which reminds me, why do we have to talk? If you want sex be prepared to talk. Remember, that communication involves listening – if you are a good listener you could probably get away with minimal talking. The purpose of talking is to establish intimacy. This is how women in particular feel intimate. Men on the other hand often feel awkward around conversation with women, especially if it is conflictual or involves feelings.

When you first started dating there was probably a lot of talking going on. You were learning about each other. Talking is a good way to find out who the other person is by what they talk about. What are their attitudes and beliefs about people, relationships and the world at large? Do you have mutual interests, what are your likes and dislikes and the list goes on. It is through this early communication that you get an expanded sense of the other person.

At least that is what's possible. The reality is (choose what fits) 1) the guy does all the talking trying to impress his date, 2) she does all the talking while the guy is figuring out how to get her home and in bed, or 3) they are both talking and so enamored with each other that neither one is really listening as they are hearing through rose-colored hearing-aids.

Obviously, these options are not a good start for effective communication in a relationship. Sooner or later it will be time to have a real conversation where both people can lay out their needs and desires. This is when you will have the opportunity to figure out what your partner wants. Indeed, this may be the first time you have an understanding of who she is and whether or not you can make this work.

Typically, men and women do not know how to have a reasonable communication when there is conflict. It is more like a fight and there is very little appreciation of who the other person is and what their needs are. If you are able to get to communicate you will be far ahead of most guys and on the way to a healthier relationship which includes . . . more sex. Yes!!!

Fights

Whether you fight a little or a lot is not important. What is important is whether or not you respect each other. Having respect will influence how you fight to some degree. Personally, the less fighting there is the happier I am. I do know couples who say they don't fight and are in big trouble. The tensions are impossible to keep underground forever and eventually they split up not even knowing why. After all, they never fought.

Conflict is a part of living. Why? Because we are two unique people who will not always want the same thing at the same time and when we are denied what we want the undeveloped part of ourselves will be reactivated and feel hurt or threatened. We will be thrown into survival mode and we will freeze, fight or go into flight.

Fortunately, we have a brain. Unfortunately, most of us forget how to use it when confronted or thwarted in our desires. Fortunately, you can learn how to use your brain when under stress.

Continuous learning

Welcome to the world of life-long-learning. Whether you are twenty, forty, or sixty years old, you are capable of learning new habits of relating and communicating. As long as you are motivated and willing to put your ego aside you can learn effective communication skills.

In a sense, the communication skills are a small but very important part of the whole process. You will learn more about yourself than anything else. You will also learn a lot about your partner as you develop your listening skills. Finally, you will come to realize that as you are better able to communicate, your relationship deepens and a whole new world opens up in which your compassion for your partner and yourself expands. Then a sense of ease enters your life as arguments decrease and sex increases. The result is a happier and more fulfilling relationship.

The feminine mystique

Feminine mystique (FM) is that mysterious power that attracts you to women and makes you want to do things for them. Modern science says it is simply pheromones that drive you into this state of diminished capacity. But hey, even when I am not in the thrall of a woman I can appreciate women in a non-desperate fashion. It seems that the feminine mystique may be more complicated than sex hormones. Whatever the full explanation, FM can be manifested with a look, a walk, a laugh, a smile, and yes, even a smell.

The FM can be intoxicating – please note that the root of intoxicating is toxic. When we are under the spell or mystery of a woman's charms we become mush balls willing to do anything for her. Fortunately, over time the spell wears off and we encounter reality. Unfortunately, when we recover our senses we discover that we are hopelessly enmeshed in a relationship and possibly with a person we can't stand.

This has happened to most guys at least once in their lifetime. Coming out of that fog is a sobering experience. Being in the fog is like being drunk. You feel high, everything is great, you are giddy and nothing bothers you. Sobering up is painful.

Unfortunately, there is no going back to that blissful and ignorant state with the same woman. So, we get drunk again with another woman and repeat the process. We all know people like that. They are in love with being in love. They are not in love with a person, just the process. In a sense, they are love addicts.

You on the other hand, because you are reading this book, are trying to deal with the reality of your girlfriend, partner or wife. You have woken up from the spell, maybe yesterday or perhaps twenty years ago, and are trying to have a relationship where each person feels appreciated and loved. Is that too much to ask? I think not.

Understanding is the booby prize

I've said it before and I'll say it again, understanding is the booby prize. There are a number of reasons for this. One, if you think you will ever understand a woman you will be sorely disappointed. Two, understanding just keeps you in your head and women hate this. They want to see your emotions. Oh, I know, you hate this. Just proves my point. Why is it women want to see, or better yet, *feel* your emotions. Even if you know this answer, odds are that you still have difficulty putting what you know into practice because you:

- Don't like to feel vulnerable emotions
- Don't want to admit having emotions
- Hate being vulnerable in front of a woman (or a man for that matter)
- Hate being wrong
- Hate even more feeling not in control of yourself or your emotions.

Even though I am stating that you can never fully understand a woman I do believe you can understand them a lot more than you presently do if you are willing to make the attempt and create some changes. This is what counts in a woman's eye.

If, on the other hand, you insist on being right and question her reality and think she is out to lunch – then you are destined for the dust bin. One day you will find yourself being tossed out like the trash. Not a fun experience according to all the men I have talked with. Some of them still think they were right. They are also very sad and do not understand what happened. This is a paradox that escapes them.

Use what works

I am loyal to my partner and loved ones. I am *not* loyal to any system of knowledge or way of doing something. I am always looking for a better way which means I need to keep my mind open. I will use whatever works in my business and in life. I recommend that you adopt this orientation as well if you want to be more effective in life and not stuck in patterns of behavior that are no longer effective – if they ever were.

How does this apply to your relationship? If you find yourself constantly trying to explain things to your wife over and over and she just doesn't get it – guess what? – you are ineffective. Your way of communicating isn't working. Acknowledge your results – minimal – and change your tactics.

This is made difficult because we want the other person to change. This is not about whether you are right or not. You may even be right but your method of communicating is not working. So stop beating your head against the wall and figure out a more effective strategy.

Hint: *Ask her what works!!*

Watch out for pride

Temper gets you into trouble, pride keeps you there.

Anon

This is a tough one. Pride is that arrogantly high self-opinion that makes everyone else want to upchuck. In relationship it shows up when this opinion of yourself will not allow you to admit making a mistake. After all, you know everything and know how others should feel and treat you. Even if you are a nice guy, admitting an error is not something you as a man do with ease.

Another word we can substitute for pride is ego. Our ego does not want to be diminished and believes (incorrectly) that admitting a mistake or lack of knowledge is akin to treasonous behavior and the punishment is death. Fearing death you shut your mouth and risk your relationship. It takes courage to face the firing squad of your partner's wrath and say, "you're right" and "I'm sorry."

You don't always get what you want, but if you try real hard, you just might get what you need (with apologies to the Rolling Stones for the paraphrasing). Wants and needs are two different things. Wants are extra and needs are fundamental (I need food and I want a chocolate sundae). You might want sex every day but only need it X times to be comfortable and feel taken care of in the relationship. You might want the Maserati but need transportation and will accept the Toyota.

When thinking about wants and needs, get your needs handled first – then work on the wants. Throughout this book we have made lists and I have stressed the necessity of compromise. It is in the examination of your wants and the other person's wants that you discover your true needs. The want is typically the ideal and the need is what works and still keeps us happy. Sometimes our want and need is identical but not often. You have to look at your life and honestly determine what is working and what is not.

When you are clear that something is not working (acknowledging the problem) you can then look to see if it is because you have a want masquerading as a need. If you hear yourself saying things like, "I have to have sex seven times a week or I will die," you can be assured that 1) you won't die, 2) you are delusional if you actually believe it and 3) this is a want disguised as a need.

When it's easy, it's easy. When it's hard, it's hell.

I have been in very difficult relationships where I stayed in way past the due date. But even in those relationships there were great times. It is no doubt why I stayed in at all. However, waiting for those great times to recycle back into the present moment was difficult and painful. Eventually, I had to ask myself if all the pain was necessary. When I was able to believe that I did not need to torture myself, then and only then, was I able to leave.

These up and down relationships are characterized by extremes. Great sex and horrible fights/arguments. Fun with other people no fun with each other. Lousy sex and great conversations, or lousy conversations and great sex. These are descriptions of unhealthy relationships where there is a quick flipping back and forth between heaven and hell and where the differences are in the extreme. A healthy relationship on the other hand is more accepting.

There was an old expression I first heard in the *est* training in the eighties, "When you're hot, you're hot, and when you're not, you're not."

The essence of this pithy statement was simple. Stop trying to explain and understand everything and just accept the state you are in.

Likewise, when in a relationship there will be moments when everything is just cruising along. You are appreciative of each other, look lovingly into each other's eyes, whisper endearments throughout the day, eat great meals together and end the evening in bed having sex. Ahh, life is good.

Then there are those days when you are cranky and she is moody. No matter what is said the other person disagrees and all you want to do is walk out, be with the guys and hustle up some hot young women and end up in bed screwing your brains out. There is nothing like a good revenge fantasy. Of course some guys act it out and then have to live with the consequences – not good.

The solution, of course, lies in your ability to communicate. However, there is a little known secret – knowing *when* to communicate. Sometimes it is best to hold your breath and count to a hundred. An example would be when she is PMS'ing. Don't try and have a conversation with a person who is stoked up on hormones. That is just a waste of time. It is also one of those hell moments (which can last a few days) that you put up with because you are committed and it isn't really her fault. Again, I must have a lot of horseshoes. I have never been with a woman where this was a problem. Oh, sometimes they were not exactly in the best of moods but it was more a reaction from being in pain or uncomfortable, and giving a backrub or fetching some tea seemed to be appreciated. I have a sneaking suspicion that when a woman is unhappy in a relationship her periods are more difficult to manage.

Always come back to love

Love is what moves you from hell into heaven. You can be in the middle of a bitter fight and the moment you connect with love all can be forgiven. Nothing is so important that you cannot stop trying to be right, cannot stop making her feel bad, cannot stop trying to get her to understand your point. *Love bears all things, believes all things, hopes all things, endures all things* (Corinthians 13:7-8).

There is nothing as freeing as that moment when you let go of the need to explain or prove or punish and realize that the person opposite you is the one you love. At that moment you are touched by grace and transcend yourself. This is one of the opportunities that exists in a relationship – learning to get over yourself. When it happens the bliss you feel in that moment makes you realize how important love is and how unimportant is fighting or being right.

Coming back to love is usually talked about in relationship to the other person. It can also be about love for yourself. When you touch into self-love, not only can you stop making the other wrong (even if they have grievously hurt you) but you can now make decisions that support your well-being and do it from a place of love rather than from a place of hate.

Say you're sorry

I talked about this before but it bears repeating. Two and a half little words – I'm sorry, go a long way to repairing and re-establishing the equilibrium in the relationship. I'm sorry is not only used when you have done a major boo-boo. It is a flexible phrase and can be used to good effect when you are sorry you are fighting, sorry you misunderstood what she was saying, sorry you forgot her Birthday . . . just testing. NEVER, ever, forget her Birthday, Valentine's Day, or your wedding anniversary.

Politeness and manners go a long way

"Mind your manners sonny." Can you see a crotchety old woman pointing her cane and scolding you for letting slip out a swear word, or being impolite, or rude? Well, she was right. Minding your manners in a relationship makes life a lot smoother. It takes out the splinters as you slide along the wooden floor of life. As you know, even a small splinter can cause an inordinate amount of grief and take forever to heal. It is the same with a careless word, comment, or inconsiderate behavior. It sticks in your partner, and if not removed quickly, is a constant irritant and reminder of the harm done. If left unattended or forgotten it can become infected and poison the body (your relationship), necessitating a trip to the doctor (marriage counselor). Save yourself some money and a lot of upset. Remove splinters quickly and say you're sorry when your manners have slipped.

On the up side of manners and politeness, when you are gracious and courteous to your partner, she feels special. We live in a high-speed/high-tech world where manners and human connection are seen as anachronistic. This is unfortunate, as many businesses have found out customers leave when they are not treated well. The same goes for you in your relationship. Treat your partner with respect, be pleasant and courteous and you will be rewarded with appreciation and loyalty. As Emily Post said, "Manners are a sensitive awareness of the feelings of others. If you have that awareness, you have good manners, no matter what fork you use."

The element of surprise

If you want to keep your relationship fun, spicy, and fresh be willing to have some surprises ready to throw into the mix. Early in our relationship my partner said, "never bore me." Whoa, that was a warning and a challenge. At least I know what is important for her.

There are two types of surprises: spontaneous and planned. For me the spontaneous ones are the easiest and they just flow from my personality. I am a great improviser and can make something wild and crazy happen in the moment which takes my partner by surprise and usually delights her. It could be dancing in the mall to muzak or throwing her on the bed and giving her a vigorous and slightly mad massage when she is in pain from sciatica.

Then there are the planned surprises. These take some thought and time to prepare but the rewards are large. Surprise meals (whether cooked by you or going out), trips (be careful with this one. Don't be the only one planning trips as she may interpret this as you taking control. Also, be absolutely sure she doesn't have any conflicting activities during that time or you will have a major problem on your hands), gifts, and tickets to events she likes. This works particularly well when they are to events she loves and knows you don't really care for.

The craziest story I was told on this topic was from one of my best friends. While in the midst of making love he casually rolls to the edge of the bed, reaches over the side and pulls out a cream pie he has hidden and then hits his lover right in the face with it. As you can imagine she was SURPRISED. Then she started laughing and they really have fun smearing the cream all over each other. I'll leave the rest of his story to your imagination but I am sure that was an experience she will never forget.

Use spontaneous surprises for everyday fun and appreciation and planned surprises for the big effect. Surprises will keep boredom out of the relationship and your wife and your life interested and interesting. If you need some suggestions in this area I recommend a great little book by Ken Tanner called *The Science of Passion, the Art of Romance*. You can order it at *www.therelationshipguy.ca/products*.

Think ally, not enemy

Just because you are having conflict does not mean your lover is the enemy. It may feel like it in the moment and that is precisely when you need to remind yourself she is your partner/wife/most important person in the world to you. If you can touch into this space while fighting you will immediately pull back, even if only a fraction, from the headlong rush into hell. When you give yourself a second's pause it then becomes possible for a rational thought to enter your mind rather than the thoughtless and automatic reactions that are controlling your interaction.

With this space you can remind yourself that you and your partner want the same thing. Yes, she actually wants the same thing – a happy and loving relationship. You may be arguing about the kids, taking out the garbage, or the in-laws – but it is always towards an end. That end is a happier state of being. You do not achieve a happier state of being by forcing someone or out-arguing them. You achieve a happier state of being by identifying what they are feeling, exploring what brought them to this state, asking what would make them happier and then sharing the same things about yourself with them. In this conversation you come to a greater understanding and appreciation of the other person's reality. You may not agree with it but you will now have a sense of how the both of you can be in a happier state. You can then take action to create this state. It may be as simple as a hug, it may be a decision to do something, it may be just listening and letting her know through accurate paraphrasing that you have heard her concerns and are not dismissing them (a classic male bad habit).

If you see your wife as an ally you will look to see where you can come to joint decisions. You will look for her perspective and opinions rather than discounting or being afraid of her viewpoint. Your partner has a lot to offer – take advantage of it.

Working hand in hand throughout life

Relationships change over time. This is the way it is. The trick is to make the relationship richer and deeper rather than disconnected and shallow. There is only one way to do this. You must be involved. You must care about what is going on in her life. The best way to show this is by communication. You would think this is obvious – it isn't. At least it is not obvious in our actions. We may know intellectually and say, of course I'm interested in the well-being of my spouse but our actions bespeak another reality. We get busy. We get focused on our work. We get tired. We are depressed with all the demands. We are angry and resentful at the miserable hand life has dealt us. There are always countless reasons and circumstances that get in the way of treating our loved ones as if we really love them.

To combat the grinding realities of life takes a *consciousness* or *awareness* of how our actions, or lack thereof, are affecting the people we say we love. This is no easy feat after a long day at work when everything went wrong and the boss was giving us a hard time. And yet, this is life. When you come home you are re-entering another world – a world you and your partner have created. It is an ongoing, living, breathing, pulsating reality. It has to be fed. Your relationship can be a bloodsucking nightmare of pain, or boredom, or a rich and vibrant reflection of all that is holy. The choice is yours.

I may have been getting a bit dramatic in that last sentence but the point is, if you tend to your garden year after year you will be rewarded with a rich harvest on an annual basis. Over time, your investment will produce richer topsoil and tending to the garden/relationship will get easier with each passing year. Yes, there will be the unexpected impositions of life: the job loss, sickness, disaster, but because you have invested wisely in the relationship you will have built up a reserve of security, trust and strength that will carry you through the hard times.

Not only does the relationship evolve just with the passage of time and events but we also age. If you are young the only way to relate to this might be to think of your parents. For those of us who are over fifty, you know what I am talking about. The ageing process itself can impose changes on the relationship some of which can be minor and some which are major. There is a good possibility that you and your wife will age differently or may have age related health concerns at different times. You have a heart attack, she has diabetes, you have prostate cancer, and she has breast cancer. These and the countless other illnesses and effects of aging will dramatically influence your life and potentially your relationship. It does not have to affect the relationship negatively if you have a strong connection but it will affect many aspects of how you do the relationship. An obvious example is after surgery. Don't expect a lot of sex. If you had prostate cancer with surgery you may not even feel like having sex again. Do you think that might change the relationship dynamics? You betcha!

I hope you get the idea. The relationship changes over time based on how we have lived in the relationship, how we have changed and how our bodies have changed. Again, the best way to navigate through these changes is through ongoing and effective communication. This will take courage as the changes may affect fundamental issues of identity. Who are you when you retire? Who are you without a sex drive? Who is your partner?

Nurturing the relationship

To continue with the garden analogy, think of yourself as the soil. Are you rich in potassium and nitrogen? Are you thick and loamy or a dry desert lacking nutrients? To have a successful garden you must have healthy and vital soil. Take the time to prepare yourself and you will shift the odds of success in your favor.

She is the seed that gets dropped into the receptive and healthy soil. What next? Seeds are delicate and need optimal conditions to grow and flourish. You need water and warmth. In the relationship you must bathe her with the necessities of life. Women are looking for the elements that will allow them to grow and a safe place for their children to blossom.

Having a job is a good thing. In other words, you must be able to provide security. This is not just financial. Not all land is perfect for growing but if you can provide emotional security, loyalty and respect, you may discover a hardy seed that can grow in these conditions (e.g., lack of money).

Love is the heat that is needed for the moisture filled seed to germinate. There is a difference between manufactured produce from hothouses and natural or organic produce grown outdoors. Not only do natural products taste better, they are hardier, having to withstand the rigors of the environment. They may not look perfect but they are real and tasty. Love is the same way. Pretending does not last long and trying to manufacture love is tasteless.

But back to our story. The seed is germinating in the healthy soil and sending out roots. This is the early stage of the relationship and root development is crucial. Because you have prepared your soul, I mean soil; it is easy for the roots to expand into you. Yes, you are being penetrated by her roots. It is at this point that many relationships end. The feeling of being enveloped or penetrated or her getting under your skin, becoming part of you, is too uncomfortable to bear. And yet, this is what it takes to have a rich relationship/garden that bears fruit.

At the same time, as the roots are diving deep into your being, the first leaves break through the soil. Oh what a happy time for the gardener. He can see that the seed has taken hold and looks at those first green shoots with delight and imagines all that will be. With leaves open to the sun, the little plant (your relationship) grows quickly strengthening day by day. These can be giddy times – the springtime of your love.

But the weather, like life is not always constant and your garden can be hit with a nasty storm that threatens to break the seedling at the base. These storms can include: another woman, discovering you have a hot tamale and you thought she was a cool cucumber as you realize that the seeds in the package were mislabeled – what a surprise! It could be in-laws (slugs) which come in the night and leave a nasty trail wherever they go. It could be birds chirping and gossiping and pecking away at the relationship, it could be any number of predators, large (deer) or small (cutworms) who have no consideration for your budding romance/garden.

Do not despair. Yes the challenges of growing a healthy plant/relationship are large but not insurmountable. You, being a wise gardener have studied (this book at least), taken workshops on gardening, and maybe even have some experience with previous gardens and know that it is important to have: a deer fence, sprays for fungi, traps for slugs (beer works great), healthy soil (self development), and a goal (a healthy relationship). You have picked your fruit well (I hope) and have done all the preparation needed to create the greatest possibility of success.

If you have done all these things you get to watch your relationship garden grow and flower throughout the summer. Maintenance of course is needed but you are past the delicate stages of springtime. The relationship is stronger and can withstand the assaults of daily living. Because you have maintained a constant vigilance for relationship destroying critters both internal and external you are rewarded with the fruits of your efforts. Happy feasting!

ICU

This one is a gem that I re-discovered recently. I was watching the movie Avatar in 3-D the week that it came out and there is a moment when the hero and the heroine gaze into each other's eyes and say, "I see you." This is a variation on the Indian tradition of saying "Namaste" which is what one says when greeting someone and means I honor or acknowledge the God within you.

In the movie, when they said this, it almost brought tears to my eyes. The reason I was so touched was the quality of the moment. They were taking time to look, really look into the other's eyes, and see the person in front of them. When you do this, connection is created. It is created for you and your partner.

It was only two weeks ago that I saw the movie and my partner and I have started a new tradition. Every day we take a few seconds, look into each other's eyes, breathe, and appreciate the other person. Then we say, "I see you." It is simple and yet the experience can be profound. It definitely makes us feel connected to one another. I highly recommend it.

Summary:

It is easy to forget the big picture when engaged in the daily battle of survival and search for happiness. We focus on the small stuff and forget what's important. If you have found a decent person, invested time and effort into the relationship and have love for your partner, keeping your eye on the ball will make life a lot easier.

Keeping your eye on the ball includes giving loving attention to your partner. You do this by taking the time to talk and listen. You engage with her when conflict arises rather than stonewalling, running away or arguing to win at all costs.

Engaging in this process is about continuous learning. It will never end because understanding the feminine reality is a never-ending process. The feminine mystique is not only mysterious but complex. If you think you understand women you are in for a big disappointment. Remember, understanding is the booby prize. Don't be a booby.

Instead, use what works and not what you think should work. Watch out for your pride as it will want to have things done the right way (i.e., your way). Making an effort to communicate and working towards understanding increases the odds that you will be appreciated and get what you need.

Ignore the relationship at your own peril. That said, sometimes shit hits the fan for no apparent reason. Even if you know the reason it will not necessarily make it better. Au contraire, it may even make it worse. Now you are a know-it-all. At these times it is better to take a big breath and know this is one of those no-win situations. A gracious exit may be all that can be salvaged in this case. And that's OK. Sometimes relationships are a pain in the ass.

While you are taking a big breath, come back to love. Realize this is one of those days where relating is difficult. Say you are sorry, if only for the fact that it is not working well today and be respectful. Politeness and manners go a long way and will help you avoid foot-in-mouth disease. Try to remember that she is your ally not the enemy.

A long-term relationship develops and matures over time. The richness of a relationship that has effective communication is a joy to live in. This partnership is made stronger every time you successfully overcome some challenge or barrier. If you can communicate then these challenges that you encounter in life are just that – challenges. They are not threats to the relationship. By nurturing your relationship you have contributed to the strength and well-being of your partner, yourself and the relationship.

That's it. I hope you have been sharing what you have learned with your partner and practicing the skill sets. I wish you well on your road to better communication, fewer arguments and more sex.

Social Media Info

For more information visit our websites:

stevenlake.com

wizeuppublishing.com

thesexformula.com

therelationshipguy.ca

talk2mehowtocommunicatewithwomen.com

Stay connected by joining us on Facebook and Twitter:

facebook.com/**HowToCommunicateWithWomen**

twitter.com/**talk2MEHowTo**

If you have any thoughts or questions please email me at:

info@**therelationshipguy**.ca

Lists and Tables

Notes

1. See Wallerstein's *The Unexpected Legacy of Divorce: A 25-Year Landmark Study* (Hyperion, 2000) and Huure's "Long-term psychosocial effects of parental divorce," *European Archives of Psychiatry and Clinical Neuroscience* 256, Number 4, (2006): 256-263.

2. Scott Haltzman, MD, clinical assistant professor in the department of psychiatry and human behavior at Brown University in Providence, R.I., and author of *The Secrets of Happy Families: Eight Keys to Building a Lifetime of Connection and Contentment.*

3. Schlaepfer T.E., Harris G.J., Tien A.Y., Peng L., Lee S., Pearlson G.D. Structural differences in the cerebral cortex of healthy female and male subjects: a magnetic resonance imaging study. *Psychiatry Res.* 1995 Sep 29; 61(3):129-35 [MEDLINE].

4. U.S. Department of Labor: Women's Share of Labor Force http://www.ebst.dk/publikationer/rapporter/gem/kap5.html. Also, BBC noted that there is a trend that will tip the scale of the wealthy, with female entrepreneurs representing 60 percent of the U.K.'s wealthiest by 2025. http://www.futuristspeaker.com/2009/06/the-coming-wave-of-entrepreneurship/

5. For a colorful graph see Larry Cahill's "His Brain, Her Brain" in *Scientific American*, May, 2005.

6. Frederikse, M.E., Lu, A., Aylward, E., Barta, P., Pearlson, G. Sex differences in the inferior parietal lobule. *Cerebral Cortex* vol. 9 (8) p896 – 901, 1999 [MEDLINE].

7. Schlaepfer T.E., Harris G.J., Tien A.Y., Peng L., Lee S., Pearlson G.D. Structural differences in the cerebral cortex of healthy female and male subjects: a magnetic resonance imaging study. *Psychiatry Res.* 1995

Sep 29; 61(3):129-35 [MEDLINE].

8. Rabinowicz T., Dean D.E., Petetot J.M., de Courten-Myers G.M. Gender differences in the human cerebral cortex: more neurons in males; more processes in females. *J Child Neurol.* 1999 Feb; 14(2):98-107. [MEDLINE].

9. The following research was found in *Phi Kappa Phi Forum 2005 (Special issue on the Human Brain)* The Essential Difference: the male and female brain. By Simon Baron-Cohen, Cambridge University.

10. See Blatchford, Peter, Ed Baines & Anthony Pellegrini, 2003; and Pellegrini, Anthony D., Peter Blatchford, Kentaro Kato & Ed Baines, 2004; and Blatchford et al. 2003 in *Qualitative Research in Children's Play: A review of recent literature* by Johan Meire at http://www.k-s.be/docs/LITERATUURSTUDIE%20SPELEN.pdf

11. Kyratzis, A. (2001). Children's gender indexing in language: From the separate worlds hypothesis to considerations of culture context and power. *Research on Language and Social Interaction, 34,* 1-14.

12. Leet-Pellegrini, Helena M. 1980. Conversational dominance as a function of gender and expertise. *Language: Social Psychological Perspectives,* ed. Howard Giles, W. Peter Robinson, and Phillip M. Smith, 97-104. Oxford: Pergamon.

13. The following list of differences were sourced from Tannen's books including: *Talking from 9 to 5: How women's and men's conversational styles affect who gets heard, who gets credit, and what gets done at work,* William Morrow and Company, New York, 1994; *You Just Don't Understand: Women and Men in Conversation.* New York: Ballantine Books, 1990; and *That's not what I meant: How conversational style makes or breaks relationships.* Ballantine Books, New York, 1986.

14. Nadler, Marjorie, and Lawrence Nadler. 1987. "The influence of

Gender on Negotiation Success in Asymmetric Power Situations." Advances in gender and Communication research, ed. by Lawrence B. Nadler, Marjorie Keeshan Nadler, and William R. Todd-Mancillas, 198-218. Lantham MD: University Press of America.

15. Fishman, Pamela. 1978. "Interaction: The work women do." *Social Problem* 24: 397 – 406.

16. Maltz, D. N., & Borker, R. A. (1982). A cultural approach to male-female miscommunication. In J. J. Gumperz (Ed.), *Language and social identity* (pp. 196-216). New York: Cambridge University Press.

17. Arliss, Laurie P. *Gender Communication*. Englewood Cliffs, NJ: Prentice-Hall, Inc., 1991.

18. To see this survey go to www.MarriageAdvice.com

19. This info is from a report by the Institute of Medicine of the National Academies that was released on March 1, 2001.

20. Risky business: explaining the gender gap in longevity. Susan P. Phillips. *The Journal of Men's Health & Gender*, Volume 3, Issue 1, March 2006, Pages 43-46.

21. These differences were found by Camarata and Woodcock on a sample of 8,000 men, women, and children. Sex differences in processing speed: Developmental effects in males and females. *Intelligence*, Volume 34, Issue 3, May 2006, Pages 231-252.

22. Gottesman, I. I. (1991) *Schizophrenia Genesis: The Origin of Madness*. New York: Freeman.

23. Garrick Bailey and James Peoples, *Essentials of Cultural Anthropology 2nd Ed.* (Wadsworth Publishing, 2010).

24. Christopher Ryan, *Evolutionary Psychology Deserves Criticism: Is rape just human nature? What about War? Sexual hypocrisy?* Published on June 24, 2009 in Psychology Today.

25. FAO. 1995. *Women, agriculture and rural development: a synthesis report of the Africa region.* Rome.

26. *Encyclopedia Britannica Online,* 2010.

27. Casey B. Mulligan. *When will women become a majority in the workforce?* Published May 6, 2009 in the NY Times blogs.

28. Doige, N. (2007). *The brain that changes itself: Stories of personal triumph from the frontiers of brain science.* New York: Penguin Books.

29. "The average American is exposed to 247 commercial messages each day." Consumer Reports Website http://www.consumerreports.org/main/detailv2.jsp?CONTENT%3C%3Ecnt_id=18759&-FOLDER%3C%3Efolder_id=18151

30. According to Alf Nucifora, an Atlanta-based marketing consultant: "Research tells us that the average American consumer is exposed to more than 600 advertising messages a day in one form or another." The Business Journal Phoenix Website http://phoenix.bizjournals.com/phoenix/stories/1997/05/05/smallb2.html

31. In the article *Practical Advice from the Union of Concerned Scientists* by Michael Brower, PhD, and Warren Leon, PhD: "The average American is exposed to about 3000 advertising messages a day, and globally corporations spend over $620 billion each year to make their products seem desirable and to get us to buy them." Union of Concerned Scientists Website http://www.ucsusa.org/publications/guide.ch1.html

32. "A conservative estimate has the average American consumer exposed to more than 850 commercial messages a day." Texas A&M University Digital Library http://dl.tamu.edu/Projects/AndersonRetailing/vol4/92Vol4No6P2.htm

33. National Health Service – UK, Mental Health Bulletin. Third report from Mental Health Minimum Dataset (MHMDS) annual returns,

2004-2009. 25th November 2009

34. Argys, Laura M. (2006). Birth order and risky adolescent behavior. *Economic Inquiry*, Volume 44, No. 2, p. 215-233.

35. I love the title of this book, *Born to Rebel* by Frank Sulloway (1997). Random House. A more recent work in 2001 is "Birth Order, Sibling Competition, and Human Behavior" in Paul S. Davies and Harmon R. Holcomb, (Eds.), *Conceptual Challenges in Evolutionary Psychology: Innovative Research Strategies*. Dordrecht and Boston: Kluwer Academic Publishers. pp. 39-83.

36. Again, see Wallerstein's *The Unexpected Legacy of Divorce: A 25-Year Landmark Study* (Hyperion, 2000) and Huure's "Long-term psychosocial effects of parental divorce," *European Archives of Psychiatry and Clinical Neuroscience* 256, Number 4, (2006): 256-263

37. See marriageadvice.com for more info on this poll.

38. Maltz, M., (1960). *Psycho-Cybernetics*. Prentice-Hall Inc. Englewood Cliffs, N.J.

39. You can read this article online. It is by E. S. Byers, "Evidence of the importance of relationship satisfaction for women's sexual functioning." *Women & Therapy*, Vol. 24, No. 1/2, 2001, pp 23-26.

40. Gottman, J., Silver, N. (1999). *The Seven Principles for Making Marriage Work*. Three Rivers Press, New York.

41. There are a number of articles of the effects of TV watching on the brain. One of the earliest was by Herbert Krugman in Brain Wave Measures of Media Involvement, *Journal of Advertising Research*, Vol. 11, number 1, February 1971.

42. Mehrabian, Albert; Ferris, Susan R. (1967). "Inference of Attitudes from Nonverbal Communication in Two Channels." *Journal of Consulting Psychology* 31 (3): 248–252.

43. These numbers were arrived at by adding the amount of emotions believed to exist from fourteen main researchers. The range was from two to eleven emotions. There is a great chart at http://changingminds.org/explanations/emotions/basic%20emotions.htm showing the theorists and the basic emotions.

44. This is from an article by Hollandsworth in *American Woman* in the May/June issue, 1995.

45. This quote is from *Friedman's Fables* (1990). The Guildford Press, New York.

46. Klohnen, E. C., & Mendelsohn, G. A. (1998). Partner selection for personality characteristics: a couple-centered approach. *Personality and Social Psychology Bulletin*, 24, 268-278.

47. Watson, D., Klohnen, E. C., Casillas, A., Nus Simms, E., Haig, J., & Berry, D. S. (2004). Match makers and deal breakers: analyses of assortative mating in newlywed couples. *Journal of Personality*, 72, 1029-1068.

48. Read this paper for an introduction on the research literature. McGee, E., & Shevlin, M. (2009). Effect of humor on interpersonal attraction and mate selection. *The Journal of Psychology*, 143 (1), 67-77. Also, for the original research see Anderon, N. H. (1968). Likeableness rating of 555 personality-trait terms. *Journal of Personality and Social Psychology*, 9, 272-279, and Craik, K.H., Lampert, M., D., & Nelson, A., J. (1996). Sense of humor and styles of everyday humorous conduct. *Humor*, 9, 273-302.

Index

Notes

Notes

Notes

STEVEN LAKE is a speaker, coach, and author of The Sex Formula: How to calculate sexual compatibility.

He is a master communicator and known by friends as "The Relationship Guy." His expert communication skills keep him connected to family, friends, colleagues and most importantly, his intimate partner.

Steven has a Doctorate in Educational Administration and a Master's degree in Counselling. He is an Adjunct Professor at the Adler School of Professional Psychology and has worked as a psychotherapist for twenty years.

Steven also conducts executive coaching and training through his company Executive Support Net and can be contacted at dr.steve@executivesupportnet.com

For relationship coaching or speaking, contact Steven at steven.lake@therelationshipguy.ca

CPSIA information can be obtained
at www.ICGtesting.com
Printed in the USA
LVOW13s0502180517

534944LV00036B/1418/P